By Survivor Science Press

I0176844

Content Warning:

This book contains accounts of domestic threat, coercive behaviour, police involvement, and references to trauma, mental health challenges, and medication. Some sections may describe emotionally intense or distressing experiences and could feel unsettling or triggering to readers. Please approach this book with care, and know that it reflects real experiences of survival, resilience, and the complex realities of navigating harmful relationships.

SURVIVING A SOCIOPATH

28 Years of Fear, Manipulation & Control

Memoir

Table of Contents

Published by Survivor Science Press

ISBN: 978-1-7637588-2-7

First Published 10 December 2025

For permission requests, write to the publisher at admin@survivorscience-press.com

Introduction: Into the Maze

⸻

24 February 2024. 10:50 p.m. I pull up outside Ava's house. The street is unnaturally still. Moths circle the streetlight, wings flickering in the pale glow across the bonnet. I cut the engine. The sudden hush presses against my ears. For a moment, I sit still, listening to the night breathe around me.

It was summer, the kind of night where the air clings warm against the skin and the crickets sing their endless chorus from the grass. House lights glowed in the distance, small squares of ordinary life where families moved through their routines — laughter, dishes, television hums. Inside my own head, though, there was nothing. Blank. The cycle was worsening, especially since I had begun working from home, pouring myself into a business he dismissed as "tapping a keyboard all day." His injury kept him idle, and my work became invisible, devalued. Yet beneath my skin an energy pulsed, a vibration so strong it felt like an engine running at full capacity, shaking with the effort of containing itself.

Six minutes earlier, at 10:44 p.m., a single line arrived on my phone: 'You or the girls come here when I'm not here, I will kill you all.'

It is not dressed in drama. It is not cloaked in bravado. It is blunt, clinical — absolute. You would expect it to strike like a blow to the chest, to knock the air from my lungs. Instead, I felt nothing — and that nothingness was its own terror. My body surviving what my mind could not yet absorb. The words are not a plea for understanding, not a question, not even an argument. They are a statement of fact, a boundary carved in fire.

I have learned to listen to the weather inside my body. The constant undercurrent in my chest, the tremor that travels through me when a door closes a fraction too hard, when a night sounds too quiet, when a voice dips just a degree too close to anger. My body knows before my mind admits it.

There had always been a pattern — words sharpened into threats, the suggestion of being hit, the constant edge of danger. But never before had it arrived in a text, never before had it carried the blunt promise of death. Twenty-seven years of this, and my body had learned its own choreography: numbness on the outside, a tornado racing inside. Nothingness was survival, but inside I was running at a hundred miles an hour, perhaps accelerated by the 100mg of Pristiq that kept me tethered. Words can wound, but silence is worse — like a pot left on the stove, lid rattling, waiting for the inevitable explosion.

I open the car door and step out, drawing in a breath I pretend is ordinary. It isn't. Breath should be easy when you are walking into your daughter's home — a place meant to hold warmth and ordinary chaos. A dog barking once, then forgetting what it was barking at. A hall light left on. The muffled sound of a TV drifting from behind a closed door.

But tonight the air feels loaded, heavy with threat, like a cyclone bending branches before it breaks. All I wanted was peace. Instead, I carry the echo of that message inside me, a line that has already rewritten the night. Only an hour earlier I had called 1800 Respect, my lifeline in the dim hours before midnight. Their voice steadied me, but the weight of danger has not lifted.

24 February 2024.

That morning the air already felt thick with trouble, a heaviness pressing against my skin before I could even name it aloud. I retreated to my therapy room, closing the door softly behind me, pretending to settle into the familiar work that usually steadies me when the world begins to tilt. I tried to stay calm, to distract myself, to keep my body from shaking out of control. Yet the tremor was already there, humming beneath the surface, waiting for the smallest spark.

The therapy room was my sanctuary. Online courses, studies, building my website — each was escape, passion, lifeline. Yet even there, a heaviness pressed down. I no longer laughed freely, barely smiled, spoke only when necessary to limit exposure to threat. Effervescence had been muffled into fatigue. My survival ritual became mechanical: breakfast, retreat to the therapy room, lunch, retreat again, dinner, bed. Sometimes a book, sometimes study outside, but always circling back to the one space where I could breathe without his shadow pressing against me.

The tension wasn't loud. It didn't announce itself with shouting or slammed doors. It crept under the threshold, wound along the carpet, curled into the corners of the couch. My husband sat in the lounge like a shadowed weight, his silence filling the house until the walls seemed to shrink. Even without words, his presence pressed against me, a constant reminder that danger doesn't always roar — sometimes it waits, patient and heavy, in the quiet.

I moved through the day on high alert, every action calculated to avoid collision: heating lunch, retreating to the therapy room, pretending to work — anything to contain the tremor in my body and preserve the fragile space between us. The hours blurred, each one taut with anticipation, each one stretching longer than it should, as though time itself had been distorted by fear.

I stayed there all day, a silent observer of my own rising panic. Dinner was already made — a small mercy in a day that offered none. With him anchored in the lounge, I slipped into the kitchen, reheated my plate, and retreated once more to the bedroom, my only sanctuary. The door clicked shut behind me, a soft but defiant barrier against the turbulence coiling inside my chest.

I sat on the edge of the bed, trying to drown out the tension with the flicker of a sitcom on the screen. My body betrayed me: racing and frozen all at once, adrenaline flooding my veins, every nerve alert, trapped in a loop I couldn't escape. The minutes stretched into hours, each one taut with anticipation, until the familiar, deliberate sound of footsteps approached in the hall — carrying with them the weight of a choice I did not want to make.

A knock. My chest tightened. I knew: unlock, or risk a door kicked in. Hands trembling, I opened it just enough to step back toward the bed, putting every inch of space between us.

He stood in the doorway, anger radiating in waves, his words like small, sharp knives. *"We need to talk."* My hand rose instinctively, a fragile shield. *"Not now. Please leave and shut the door."*

It didn't stop him. His tone edged closer to threat: *"If you shut me out again, I'll kick the door down."*

Fear and freeze collided, my body screaming while my mind calculated. I told him I'd call the police if he didn't leave. Still, he lingered, a dark presence rooted to the doorway.

I didn't want escalation, didn't want confrontation. My hand hovered over the phone, reaching for the lifeline I knew too well: 1800 Respect.

Relief came in fragments as I spoke to the operator, her voice a tether of calm pulling me back from the edge of thunder. The line stayed open, her cadence steady, echoing every tremor beneath my words. It wasn't that the danger vanished; it was that fear now had a witness, someone who refused to pretend it was nothing. Being seen made the chaos one degree more survivable. He stepped back, leaving the doorway, and the room suddenly felt larger, the storm receding by a fraction.

I slipped out of bed, careful not to make a sound, every muscle locked in the kind of alertness that makes silence roar. Dressing quickly, I moved with the practiced economy of someone who has a ritual I had practiced silently, muscle memory guiding each move.

The operator guided me with quiet, practical questions — What's the plan? Where are the essentials? What feels safest? I answered with the careful tempo I've learned: I have an escape bag in the car. I need my laptop. I want the charger, and a few crucial documents.

I edged toward the open door, feet wide enough to steady against the surge of fear rising in my throat. He was there, halfway down the hallway, a silhouette of heat and expectation. I paused, muscles attuned for the cue that would let me pass without turning the hall into a battlefield. Timing was everything — the breath I took before stepping forward, the way my palm pressed flat against the wall to steady the tremor threatening to bloom into something louder than a whisper, something that could ignite the night.

In the back room, the laptop waits like a practical talisman, a fragile symbol of control in a life where control feels slippery, dangerous, and easily stolen. I take it in my hands, along with the charger, knowing my escape bag and the few documents that matter most are already tucked in the car. Each item is not a trophy but a deliberate choice, a small holdfast against the night's unpredictability. I don't glance over my shoulder in fear so much as in vigilance — a habit honed by years of living inside a weather system I cannot predict but have learned to anticipate.

Retracing my steps down the hallway, every movement becomes a negotiation. Each step past him is measured: distance maintained, body primed for flight, eyes fixed forward, breath held taut like a thread stretched between two points. The silence between us is charged, a wordless exchange of momentum — a glance that might become gesture, a touch that could ignite escalation. Time slows in the way it does when fear wants to sprint. I move with the precision of someone threading a needle through silk, mindful of every inch where catastrophe could slip in if I falter.

I reach the car, and relief arrives sharp, almost cruel, in the moment I sink into the seat. My shoulders drop as if a weight has finally slid off them. The engine's purr is a mercy, a reminder that machines can be kind when the heart is unsteady. The operator, steady as ever, cuts through the fog with practical clarity: she can stay on the line or fade back if the danger subsides. I tell her to stay; I tell her I'm not ready to release the hold she has on the moment. Her voice travels through the phone like warmth through a conductor, carrying calm into a night otherwise wired with fear.

I breathe — watching the numbers glow on the dash, counting the rhythm of my lungs as they rise and fall, a heartbeat's metronome that refuses to let panic dictate the pace. Ten minutes down the road, memory surfaces with the sterile sting of truth: my anti-depressants, the pharmacological anchor I've depended on to steady my nerves, missing in the way a familiar friend vanishes just when I need them most. The realisation lands cold, but before despair can take root, the operator senses I am out of danger. She asks if she is still needed. I pause, then let her go.

I call Ava first. My voice is steady enough to form the words, but beneath them runs a tremor, the kind that betrays itself in the pauses between syllables. *"I'm on my way,"* I tell her. Outside the car window, the wind whistles against the glass, and I hear myself the way a person does when they're not sure if the next breath will be a sob or a sentence.

I keep my eyes fixed on the road, instructing Siri to dial Mia. Her response is a different kind of ache — the familiar distance that arrives when fear makes even close kin cautious, when concern hardens into something quieter, flatter. Her voice carries an exhaustion I know too well, a tiredness born not of the hour but of the years. It is the sound of someone who has run out of softness, who has chosen safety over sympathy, who asks not out of care but out of a need to protect herself from whatever turmoil she assumes might follow. In this family, fatigue has replaced curiosity, and words land with the muted thud of people who have learned to ration compassion just to survive the day.

I tell her I'm not home, that I'm heading to Ava's, at least for tonight. She doesn't ask about peace or safety in the long view; she asks only about the surety of the moment, the algebra of risk and relief.

Ava's house comes into view with a halo of porch light, the quiet hum of a fridge that has learned to purr in the late hours. There is no fanfare — no trumpets, no chorus of neighbours. Just a door opening, a figure stepping into the light, a hug that feels more like shelter than greeting, unexpected in the history of our relationship.

I show her the message, the blunt line that has carved a scar into the soft tissue of tonight: *"Mum, you need to call the police. That's not okay."* Her words aren't loud; they are clinical in their honesty, the kind of truth you need when you're still listening for the echo of fear's footsteps in the hall. If Ava hadn't told me to call the police, I doubt I would have made that call. I had no idea that this single moment — this quiet insistence — would set in motion a chain of events larger than either of us could see.

We sit at the kitchen table, a surface that has carried its share of heavy conversations, its wood clattering softly under the weight of truth. The police are called. The dispatcher's voice returns with the same steady efficiency as the 1800 Respect operator, but now it carries the gravity of official presence. When the officers arrive, their faces are drawn in lines of routine and duty, their composure a shield against the tremors of a life lived on the edge of danger.

I follow them to the table, my legs shaking, small and frantic, like a mouse caught in the grip of flight. They arranged themselves with quiet precision: the male officer steady at the far end, the female officer to my left, pen poised, questions deliberate. Ava sits to my right, her presence a fragile anchor. I speak carefully, my voice taut with the need for accuracy. Each statement was read back, corrections made with the weight of responsibility. Truth had to be exact, even when fear blurred the edges — every word a tightrope between memory and survival. They listen, record, and ask again, ensuring nothing is lost. Hours pass in this rhythm of question and answer, each pause deliberate. The officers remain patient, their steadiness a quiet support against the storm that has consumed my evening.

They tell me a unit has already been sent to my home. They explain, without dramatics but with weight in every word, that my life has been assessed as at risk. A police-issued intervention order is in place. Until court, they say, it will hold — a boundary enforced not just by will but by law.

I feel my chest lift in a subtle way at the word *safe*, a micro-relief running beneath my ribs. Around one, maybe two in the morning, as the officers collect their things to leave, they tell me it is okay to return home. He is in custody. The word *custody* echoes in my body longer than I expect — strange, heavy, almost foreign. Relief tries to seep in, but it is muted, hollow, heavy in my limbs, as though I have been emptied of energy rather than restored.

I stay with my daughter a little longer. We play a round of golf, small laughter threading through the tension. She offers for me to stay, her voice a gentle anchor, but I need my own bed. My own space. Not triumph, not victory, but the quiet knowledge that I can move again, that the edges of danger have temporarily receded.

When I return home, relief arrived quietly, a loosening in my chest, a whisper that said: you survived, for now. My conscious mind knows it is safe, but my body is still cataloguing every possibility, every footstep that has led me here.

Relief, yes — but emptied relief. Exhausted relief. The kind that leaves you hollow enough to notice the texture of fear still clinging to your skin.

Returning home in the small hours, the air was cooler but still heavy with memory. I collapsed into bed, exhausted beyond fear — the kind of exhaustion that earns only a few hours of quiet. The blankets wrap around me in a soft, familiar way, promising warmth even as my nerves continue to tremble in their private language. It isn't sleep that comes; it's a pause, a temporary cease-fire that allows the mind to settle long enough to tell the body what it needs to know: *you've earned a point of stillness, even if the clock hasn't released you yet.*

That stillness, though, fractures into raw awareness when I glance at the bedside table and see my anti-anxiety pills missing. Annoyed, I begin a search that feels absurd, almost like a scavenger hunt unfolding in the dark. I move through drawers, cupboards with care. In the bin, an empty packet first, then blister packs scattered like casualties, the acrid scent sharp in my nostrils — proof that even the smallest lifelines can vanish, manipulated by circumstance or intent. At the bottom, nothing. The pills are gone.

A wave of resignation tugs at my chest, and I almost give in. Then halfway down the hallway, a flicker of recognition sparks — an epiphany. The empty packet isn't tonight's; it's last week's. Determined, I pivot back, moving with quiet insistence toward the bottom drawer of the dresser. There they are. Nestled in the dark, the white of the box glimmers faintly in the half-light — tactile relief, reassurance. My body exhales tension I hadn't realised it was holding. These tablets are more than medication; they are a signal that I can still reach for stability in the middle of chaos, that I can gather myself again. Relief was fleeting; the knock that followed shattered it before it could settle.

The clock's hands creep toward 3:00 a.m. Then 3:30. At 4 a.m., a knock shatters the fragile quiet. Two police officers stand at the door, calm but deliberate. Behind them is Ex, moving cautiously, aware of boundaries he is no longer allowed to cross. I am guided to the back room, the walls closing in softly around me as I sit with the officer, going over the conditions of the intervention order. Every word lands carefully, measured, my pulse slowing and tightening in rhythm with comprehension. They reassure me he has been cooperative in custody, that there is no danger while the order is in place.

Nearly an hour later, the officers prepare to leave. I rise, checking that Ex has gathered everything he needs. My stomach tightens when I realise he is leaving without his medication. I offer it to the police. They shake their heads gently — personal belongings, untouchable. The pills stay behind, a small, uneasy absence. They tell me he will be staying at the footy oval up the road, just outside the 200-metre restriction zone. There is nothing more they can do.

I nod, thank them, and return to bed. The house settles around me, but the tension does not. The night stretches on, a living thing refusing to be contained. My body remains alert, muscles humming with the memory of the hours just passed, reminding me that safety is never simple, never final.

About half an hour later, my phone vibrates — a number I don't recognise. My chest tightens before I even answer. It's him. His voice slips through the line, low and edged: *"What did you go and do that for?"*

I clamp my jaw, my fingers curling around the phone as if it could anchor me. *"You're not supposed to call me,"* I say, the words deliberate, steady. I've promised my daughter I would uphold the order, that any contact would be reported. My body hums with the memory of every warning signal I've learned to trust — the tone, the timing, the way danger disguises itself as grievance.

I call the police. They've only just returned to the station, twenty to twenty-five minutes away. The minutes crawl, each one stretched thin by anticipation. At 6 a.m., they arrive again. The officers move with the same quiet precision, and I give an additional statement, every word measured, every pause recorded. Ex is taken to the holding cell to wait out the weekend until the courts open on Monday, 26 February 2024.

The walls seemed to loosen their grip, as if the house itself had unclenched with me as the officers leave, but I remain alert, muscles still taut, the weight of vigilance pressing along my spine. Even now, even after the legal steps are taken, the body remembers — the rhythm of fear, the texture of tension, the tiny, constant signals that whisper: *stay present, stay careful, keep the line drawn.*

The next morning arrives not with a shout but with an ordinary sun that makes the kitchen look different, the way a photograph changes colour when you tilt it toward the light. I lie in bed long enough to feel the room steady around me, to hear the sound of the day pressing at the edges of the door. Then I rise, not with a roar but with a slow, deliberate intention: I will face this day with a new grammar of safety, with the knowledge that I've proven I can act on what I know to be true, even when fear insists that truth is a rumour.

Monday. His case has been heard, the courtroom still echoing with the remnants of procedure, and he is out on bail. No money. No plan. No way to get home. And then my phone rang — the storm returning, disguised as need.

It was him, outside the courthouse, he stood at a payphone, calling me again — the same violation that had landed him in holding cells only hours before. Lessons ignored, boundaries mocked. If this was not the action of a sociopath, what was? He had always relied on me to do everything, to manage every detail of his life. Only recently had I opened my own bank account, breaking free from the coercive threats that once forced me to hand over money for drugs. He could never hold funds; they slipped through his fingers before payday arrived. Now, hearing his voice through the tinny speaker, I felt unsettled, knowing he was on his way back to town, knowing the storm was circling again. His voice coming through the payphone, the request was simple, urgent: money so he could make it home. My chest tightened at the familiar pull — the old reflex of wanting to help, to fix — but my body was alert, taut. I transferred $200, watching the numbers confirm, each digit a small assertion that I was still in control of this moment, still standing upright while the world outside remained precarious.

He caught the train to the police station to collect his mobile, a small logistical step that felt like a test of my patience, a reminder of the way he could ripple through my life even when absent. Then the text arrived: *"Ha, if ok to put 20 on the card please as it cost 120 for a taxi."*

I read it slowly. My stomach churned, my body leaning forward with the weight of calculation. I had done the math, traced the distance, considered the routes.

It should have cost $70. Not $120. My fingers hovered before I tapped out the reply: *"No, it should have cost $70."*

The text was more than money. It echoed a familiar pattern — small manipulations, testing boundaries, asserting presence through obligation. My body felt it instantly: micro-tremors, jaw tightening, heart rate rising. These weren't new sensations; they were rehearsals from childhood carried forward into adulthood.

The night's events did not arrive as an isolated event but as part of a weather system that began long before the driver's seat warmed up on Ava's street. The questions that hover — what prepared me to recognise danger and yet stay present long enough to get to safety? — are not new. They are echoes of a childhood that taught me to read faces and voices with a precision that felt like a sixth sense, a survival tool that could also become a trap if used in the wrong way.

Fear moved through me like static — unpredictable, charged, sometimes indistinguishable from Ex himself. My regulation has always been tied to his moods — testosterone rising, aggression spilling, energy he cannot contain firing off at me. Childhood taught me to be small, to obey, to silence my emotions. Don't rock the boat. Don't expect rescue. Don't complain. Treat others how you want to be treated — I tried, I tried hard, but it was never enough. That conditioning is part of a larger arc, a generational liability. It is not just personal; it is societal. Fear passed down like inheritance, silence embedded in family architecture, vulnerability woven into the fabric of survival.

In the small hours of that night, I sense the persistence of a family script I have learned to perform without thinking: the careful negotiation of fear, the insistence on calm even when the heart hammers, the habit of smoothing over a moment so the room doesn't combust. My childhood memory returns in fragments. A kitchen inadvertently loud with laughter that couldn't quite mask a trembling undercurrent. A parent who could soothe one moment and then slip into turmoil the next. A sibling who learned to vanish into a room at the first sign of danger, as if disappearances were a universal remedy.

I recall performing each unwritten norms that demanded a certain kind of behaviour: smile when you wanted to shout; respond with politeness when your body screamed for space; perform vulnerability in a way that invited care even when you were already depleted. It wasn't about cruelty or intent. Later, those same unwritten rules made it easier for others to control me — I already knew how to silence myself, how to comply, how to disappear into someone else's needs. It was about pattern — how fear becomes a familiar language, used to keep a family intact even as the people inside it are quietly, stubbornly rearranged by forces larger than themselves.

The early signs of manipulation weren't loud; they were cumulative. They arrived as small adjustments in tone, the speed of a conversation, the way a decision was framed as a moral obligation rather than a shared choice. There's a moment I carry with me — the way a parent's voice could soften into warmth one night and harden into demand the next, the way affection could arrive with an apology that never quite explained what needed repair. I learned to measure approval by the smile that followed compliance, to interpret silence as a warning that my own voice had stepped out of line.

These patterns didn't exist in a vacuum. They grew out of a family system where safety was negotiated, never guaranteed. The adults around me managed drama in ways that protected appearances — keeping the peace even if it meant masking pain, masking fear, masking truths that could destabilise a fragile balance. I absorbed those habits the way a child learns to ride a bicycle: push off carefully, balance, look ahead, don't blink, keep moving. I didn't learn to ride toward danger; I learned to ride away from it, steering through tight turns with the sense that if I paused too long, the space would close in.

And yet, within that same soil of fear, a stubborn seed grew: resilience. It wasn't loud or dramatic. It was the steady pull to rise again after a night when you were sure you had exhausted every way to endure. It was the memory of being seen, even in ordinary moments of a childhood without a full map, and choosing to trust that your body could sense danger even when your mind rationalised a smile as enough. It was the ability to recognise when fear was not a signal to run but a signal to pause, to listen, to prepare.

I learned to read the subtle cues — a tightened jaw, a rapid swallow, a pause that lingered in the air before a sentence landed with weight. I learned to translate those cues into small, practical acts of protection: step back from a conversation, choose a different room, hold my gaze steady when an adult's gaze tilted toward blame or shame. These were not heroic acts in the storybook sense, but they were acts of survival — the kind that accumulate quietly, until the ordinary becomes possible again.

The seeds of manipulation I carry forward are not stains on character but reflections of a world that taught me to adapt — to be helpful, agreeable, useful, in ways later weaponised by someone who read need as if it were a map he could hold in his hands. The person I would eventually marry — Ex — arrived with a certainty and presence that felt like shelter, a presence that promised steadiness even as it carried a risk invisible until I found myself pulling away from the same room I had always known.

This foreshadowing is not a forecast of doom. It is a careful note about who I had been long enough to know how a mind can bend to fear without intending harm. It is about how a partner can become a teacher of manipulation by accident, and how a life can be shaped by the weight of another person's mood, yet still leave space for courage to take root. Looking back now from the night's quiet after the chaos, I see the pattern not as a single flaw but as a system: a choreography in which I learned to breathe at the pace of another's need, to pause my own long enough to let someone else feel seen, to let fear shape my choices more than my own compass did.

That recognition is the spark — the moment survival becomes awareness, and awareness becomes agency. The awakening that there is a longer arc to this story than a single night's fear and a single act of escape. It will be the slow, painstaking work of naming the patterns I learned to imitate and the acts of care I learned to prioritise for myself. It will be a practice of turning the attention I gave to another's mood back toward my own safety and autonomy. It will be a reclaiming of space I can call mine — body, breath, voice, time, and truth.

Central questions rise: *How did I end up here? How did I survive?* If you had asked me a year ago whether I believed love could turn dangerous and still feel, at its best moments, like shelter, I would have hesitated. I would have said love can bruise, heal, complicate, and surprise — sometimes all at once. I would have believed in the best of people, in the possibility that a partner could be both devoted and flawed in the same breath. I would have described safety as a given — like a door that locks itself, a house that keeps its own quiet corner.

The truth of the night challenges that belief. Danger does not always shout; sometimes it whispers with a voice that sounds like care, like concern, like a request for closeness that doesn't feel like a threat until the room shifts and the world you thought you shared belongs to someone else. Survival is not a single act; it is a practice, a repetition of choices that test your willingness to name fear, to locate your boundary, to act even when every impulse says to stay put.

So I ask myself again, with stubborn honesty:

First, how did I end up here? The answer is not a single event but a map drawn in memory. A history of trading voice for calm, of reading moods like weather fronts, of accepting realities that fit someone else's needs even when they did not fit mine. It is the erosion of certainty — the way a trusted memory can be reorganised by a single sentence, the way perception can be reframed by a voice that sounds sure even when your body sounds alarm. It is the recognition that I believed in change more than I believed in my right to safety, that I interpreted mood swings as vulnerability instead of red flags, that I did not yet know how to translate fear into a boundary strong enough to stop harm.

Second, how did I survive? I survived because I learned to act with precision and care, to assemble small acts into a larger pattern of self-preservation. I reached out to support networks who did not judge but stood with me — Ava, Mia, 1800 Respect, the police. I trusted the sense my body kept when my mind was slow to accept. I moved toward a plan even when fear tried to redefine a plan as a trap. I kept a bag in the car, not as an exit prize but as a promise to myself that I would not wait for a worse moment to leave. I learned that survival is not just avoiding harm; it is claiming the right to be safe in the ordinary hours that follow, to wake in a place you recognise as yours, to rest without needing permission to breathe.

The night ends with a doorway shifting in meaning. I leave a space I once called home and enter a future uncertain — not because danger lurks in every moment, but because it demands a different kind of courage. A courage that asks me to rebuild trust, re-educate my nervous system, and redefine what safety means in the days ahead. The questions will not disappear, but they will be reframed. They will not trap me; they will guide me toward a life that belongs to me again — a future not borrowed, not conditional, but mine.

The next chapter will peel back the layers that made this possible: the childhood terrain shaping my perception of safety and belonging, the conditioning teaching me to read danger where others saw ordinary life, and the patterns that later left me vulnerable even as I longed to believe in the best of people. It is not a tale of blame but a map of roots — an honest look at where fear first took hold and how resilience began to grow in its shadow, steady and unassuming. If survival has a timetable, Chapter 2 is where the clock begins to tick toward a life that no longer bends to fear but meets it with steadier breath, clearer vision, and a more grounded sense of self.

Closing note This chapter begins the journey from the night's storm into the work of healing. It holds the raw, intimate truth of fear made practical and the seeds of strength that will take root as the pages turn. The path ahead is not a single bright line but a corridor of decisions, each one laying down a step toward reclaiming safety, autonomy, and the full sense of self I deserve. The maze remains real — but so, increasingly, does the map I will draw to find my way out, a map that insists survival is not the end of the story but the beginning of becoming whole.

Chapter 1: Roots of Vulnerability – Childhood & Conditioning

———

The White Shoes

I can still see them — white slip-on shoes, bright enough to catch sunlight and bounce it back at me. They were the kind of gift that made my whole body light up, a moment where I felt singled out, chosen, noticed. I slipped them on and felt different — taller, as though I had stepped into a version of myself I'd been waiting to become.

My nanna was outside with my brother and pop, planting zucchini seedlings in the soft soil. The smell of wet earth and cut grass clung to the air. I raced toward them, eager to show them my new treasure, heart lurching in that innocent way only childhood joy can pull out of you.

But when I arrived, instead of excitement, I got a wall.

"Go home, you'll get them dirty."

The words hit harder than reason would justify. My chest tightened instantly, the way a child's body does when belonging is suddenly revoked. I remember standing there, toes pressing into the backs of my new shoes, wishing the ground would soften beneath me.

In that moment, I learned that joy could be inconvenient. That innocence could be met with irritation. That my excitement didn't fit the emotional climate of others.

It wasn't about the dirt — it was about the message underneath:

You are interrupting something. You don't belong in this moment.

I carried that sensation — the sharp contraction around the ribs, the cheeks warming with embarrassment, the impulse to retreat and make myself smaller — far longer than I carried those shoes.

Years later, in my marriage, the same pattern appeared like déjà vu I didn't want: joy dismissed as childish, excitement deemed excessive, pleasure treated as frivolous or self-indulgent. Affection became a reward delivered unpredictably, and withheld with precision. The emotional rhythm was eerily familiar.

When kindness was offered, my body reacted as though it was a rare, startling event. I remember walking into the police station after yet another IVO breach. I stood at the counter, numb from rehearsing facts for the report. The officer serving me said something ordinary, but gentle — a softness I hadn't heard in years.

I burst into tears.

When I entered the interview room, still shaken, I told my case officer, "I don't even know why I'm crying."

He looked at me and said quietly, "It's because someone was nice to you."

My body understood him before my mind did.

Kindness had become foreign currency.

The white shoes were the first time I learned what it felt like to have joy contradicted by rejection. In adulthood, that contradiction became the emotional backbone of a life where affection was rationed and I clung to scraps of kindness like proof that love could still exist.

The Card Game

Nan's house always smelled of linen and old timber — the kind of scent that carried safety even when the dynamics inside didn't. The card table was set up near the window, sunlight spilling across the surface in gold patches. My brother and I were playing, shuffling cards with the clumsy confidence of children.

He cheated.

And I did what I believed was right — what I had been taught to do.

I told the truth.

But instead of fairness or correction, I got a name tossed like a pebble with too much force:

"Pip squeak."

The laughter that followed sealed the lesson.

My body lit up with humiliation — cheeks burning so hot I wished I could disappear behind the chair, throat tightening in that trapped way the nervous system reacts when safety dissolves.

It wasn't just teasing. It was the announcement that my voice was laughable. Exaggerated. Too small to carry authority.

But beneath the sting was another truth, stubborn and unyielding:

I still believed honesty mattered. Even if no one clapped for it.

That value rooted itself inside me, steady as bone.

In adulthood, this moment became the foundation for a different kind of pain. When gaslighting entered my marriage, the pattern clicked into place like an old wound reopening:

my truth questioned, twisted, mocked, minimised.

The child called "pip squeak" became the woman whose reality was constantly reinterpreted by someone who feared accountability.

My nervous system recognised the old pattern before my mind did — the shallow breaths, the instinct to justify myself, the automatic shrinking even when I knew I was right.

That day at the card table wasn't small.

It was training.

It was instruction.

It was a warning delivered in a joke:

Your truth will not be welcomed.

And for years, I lived out the script exactly as it had been written.

The Dinner Table

There was a different kind of lesson waiting at my mum's dad's house. The dinner table was a place of clattering cutlery, sharp laughter, and the thick scent of potatoes and roast meat. Conversation moved in waves, and like any child eager to join in, I spoke when my pop asked a question.

I answered simply, openly — wanting to be part of the connection happening around that table.

But instead of acknowledgment, I was corrected.

"You didn't say 'excuse me.'"

A moment later, my brother spoke without the phrase.

He was not corrected.

The unfairness carved itself into my awareness with surgical precision.

My stomach dropped.

My hands went still on my lap.

I understood something before I had the language for it:

His voice had permission.

Mine had rules.

The dinner table became the blueprint for a hierarchy I would later walk into in adulthood — one where men were indulged, forgiven, understood, while women were expected to be polite, controlled, grateful, quiet.

My nervous system learned to anticipate scrutiny.

My identity learned to bend.

Research today describes this as gendered social conditioning — a form of early attachment distortion where children internalise who is allowed space and who must earn it. But back then, it was just a feeling:

invisibility dressed as etiquette.

Years later, I found myself in relationships where my voice was the one corrected, analysed, dissected. Where my feelings were too much, my needs were inconvenient, my words were policed, while his behaviour slid across the surface untouched.

The dinner table taught me that fairness was conditional.

Adulthood taught me that injustice often feels familiar long before it feels wrong.

The Belief

These childhood moments may look small in isolation — white shoes, a card game, a dinner table. But the body doesn't categorise experiences as "big" or "small."

It categorises them as *safe* or *unsafe*.

Seen or *dismissed*.

Welcomed or *tolerated*.

Each experience left a mark, a subtle but persistent shift in how I perceived myself.

I grew up with a quiet, unspoken belief that boys were inherently more valued. Not because anyone declared it, but because the rules of engagement said so in a hundred tiny ways:

My joy dismissed.

My truth mocked.

My voice corrected until silence felt safer."

My body stored these lessons in muscle and breath, shaping my early attachment patterns. I learned to seek approval instead of expecting it. I learned to earn affection instead of receiving it freely. I learned to over-function, over-perform, over-prove.

So I entered adulthood trying to outrun that hierarchy by outperforming it.

I drove forklifts.

Reversed miniature trucks.

Worked in roles few women held.

Not for love of the work, but for proof I was equal — or better.

Every achievement was a rebuttal to childhood.

Every skill a counter-argument.

But beneath the competence was a wound shaped like a question:

Am I enough yet?

Abusers sense that question like sharks sense blood.

My need to prove my worth became a doorway they walked through easily.

They alternated between validation and withdrawal, praise and rejection, mirroring the emotional choreography of my childhood.

And my body responded exactly as it once had:

tight chest, breath held hostage, shrinking around discomfort, trying to appease, trying to earn warmth.

Those small childhood moments didn't just shape my personality — they primed my nervous system for relational instability.

They prepared me to tolerate inconsistency, to normalise crumbs of affection, to endure environments where my needs were overlooked.

The child who learned to make herself smaller grew into the adult who accepted love that required shrinking.

Why These Memories Matter

Looking back, I see the through-line clearly — each moment a thread in the tapestry of attachment, belonging, and identity:

Equality revealed itself as negotiable. Affection arrived only in fragments. Truth carried consequences. Joy was unwelcome.

These weren't isolated lessons — they were the architecture of my nervous system.

A blueprint for how I would interpret love, safety, connection, and rejection.

In psychological terms, these experiences shaped core schemas — deeply rooted beliefs about self-worth, relational expectations, and emotional safety. In body terms, they shaped autonomic responses — the tightening, freezing, appeasing, and collapsing that would later surface in trauma bonds.

But here's the part that matters most:

They also shaped my resilience.

Even in those moments — white shoes, card game, dinner table — something in me held onto truth, joy, fairness. Something in me recognised when something wasn't right, even if I couldn't articulate it. Something in me stored a quiet promise that someday, I would reclaim the voice that was minimised.

Childhood didn't just plant wounds — it planted wisdom.

Closing: The Adult Pattern Hidden in Childhood Moments

The moments etched into my childhood were not accidents. They were early drafts of the emotional landscape I would later navigate in adulthood — attachment systems shaped by invisibility, approval-seeking, and inconsistent affection.

These memories, raw and unfiltered, reveal how a person becomes vulnerable to manipulation without ever knowing they're being primed for it. Not because they are weak, but because they learned to survive by adapting to unpredictability.

The child who learned not to take up space became the adult who apologised for taking any. The child who was mocked for truth became the adult who was gaslit for it. The child who learned joy was unwelcome became the adult who stopped celebrating herself. And the child who learned boys were 'better' became the adult who worked twice as hard for half the recognition.

But the story doesn't end there.

Because the body also remembers what it needed — fairness, truth, joy, belonging.

And those unmet needs are the very keys that lead us back to healing.

This chapter isn't about blame — it's about mapping the roots.

Because understanding the past isn't dwelling in it;

it's reclaiming the parts of you that were never nurtured,

never celebrated,

never heard.

These memories don't define me.

They inform me.

They clarify who I became — and who I am no longer willing to remain.

Formative Incidents Shaping Self-Worth

Childhood is often remembered in fragments — the smell of tea cooling in a cup, the scrape of a chair against linoleum, the way silence can feel louder than words. For me, those fragments carry weight. They are not just memories; they are the scaffolding of my self-worth, the places where shame and inadequacy first took root. My body protected me at seven by silencing me, but it also carried me forward. That survival instinct, though painful, was proof of my strength.

The Cup of Tea

It was 2 p.m., the air neither hot nor cold, the kind of afternoon that should have felt ordinary. I sat at the dining table in my parents' kitchen, Dad to my right, Mum across from me. We were finishing our cups of tea when Mum began talking about her friend Kylie, lamenting that Kylie's adopted daughter, Jen, no longer spoke to her. "Poor Kylie," she said, shaking her head.

Heat rose in my body, flushing my face, a burn I could barely contain. I blurted out, "Poor Jen."

In the memory, the kitchen settles into a still frame. The kettle's hiss becomes a drumbeat you can hear in your bones. Jen's name lands in the room like a pebble dropped into a still pond. Jen—someone I once imagined as a bully, someone who wore a hardness that felt almost sculpted into her bones. She had older brothers, one of them unsafe to be around, and I learned early to listen for footfalls in the hallway, to count breaths when the door opened. One night, Mum insisted I stay at Kylie's house. I didn't want to, but at seven years old, I said nothing. Silence was my survival.

That night, in the bedroom I shared with Jen, the memory erupts in the air like steam escaping a radiator. We were both seven. Details are a quiet, dangerous thing, and I won't lay them bare here with the bluntness of a confession that could harm someone else or shame me anew. What I can say is this: my body betrayed me with a heat that pooled in my chest, a tightness around my ribs, a breath snagging in my throat. I learned that days could tilt into a night that you could not tell anyone about, not because you were forbidden to speak, but because you learned to keep the sound of your own shaking inside your mouth.

Home the next day became an inventory of nerves. I did not want to talk to anyone. Not even to tell the truth of what happened. Because telling it felt like inviting the world to confirm what I already believed about myself: that I was not safe, that I did not matter, that there was a wrongness in me that needed to be hidden away. The memory stayed with me as if someone had stitched it into the lining of my clothes. When I wore my clothes again, the material carried a weight that wasn't about fabric but about shame—shame that can travel through time and arrive with the exact same heat as it did at seven.

Decades later, sitting at that same kitchen table with my parents, I tried to speak. "Bad things happened there," I said. "I was abused the night of your mum's funeral." The words felt like a tremor in the air, a sentence spoken in a room that suddenly shifted its gravity. Dad stayed silent, his face unreadable, a map of years glitched into silence. Mum hissed across the table, "You weren't there, you were at your Aunty's."

My fists tightened, heat surged through me again. "I know exactly where I was," I said, voice trembling but steady. I left soon after, offering cool goodbyes, my body vibrating with the effort of holding myself together.

That moment taught me that even when I spoke truth, it could be denied. My body had protected me at seven by silencing me, and at forty it trembled with the same instinct. The lesson was clear: vulnerability was dangerous, honesty could be erased, and self-worth was fragile when those closest to you refused to see.

The Bonfire

Years later, my marriage was unraveling. My mother-in-law was staying with us, a figure in the background who carried her own weather—cool distances and sharp remarks that landed like stones on glass. One night I walked toward the bonfire where she and my husband stood. The air tasted of smoke and damp wood, of the summer not yet ready to end. Grief pressed against me, heavy and uncontainable. I began to cry, unable to hold back the flood.

Her response was swift: "Time to go." She left me standing there, stunned, the flames flickering against my face, a halo of orange and ash that burned into my memory. The sting wasn't only in her words but in the space she created between what I felt and what I was allowed to show. I stood there, the heat leaping along my skin, the tears traveling down my cheeks in a way that felt both urgent and useless.

I shared the moment with a therapist friend later, someone who held space without judgment. "You can't expect your behaviours from someone else when they're not capable. Accept them for who they are." The sentence landed in the room with the weight of an anchor. It was a grounding, not a reconciliation. It was a reminder that love and care can be conditional, that the architecture of a relationship can fail to bear the load of one person's weather.

It was a lesson I had been learning since childhood—that others might not meet me where I was, that my vulnerability could be met with dismissal. My body remembers the sting: the hollow chest, the ache in my throat, the way tears felt wasted, the way a confession could vanish in the heat of a reply. Each dismissal reinforced the belief that my needs were too much, my emotions inconvenient. Self-worth became tied not to my own truth but to the capacity of others to hold it—and too often, they could not.

School Years

At eight years old, school was another battlefield. Among friends, I never felt truly included. If someone was going to be teased or embarrassed, I knew it would be me. Mum's mantra echoed in my ears: "Treat others the way you want to be treated." I tried, I tried so hard. But the values she gave me didn't line up with reality.

Manners mattered more than feelings. Compliance mattered more than authenticity. I was told to put others first, to silence myself, to never interrupt. Yet others did not follow those rules. Confusion settled in my body—a tightening in my stomach, a heaviness in my chest. How was I supposed to feel safe if I felt I didn't matter?

By thirteen, the fear of rejection was embedded in me. High school was harsher than primary. I wasn't popular; even among my "misfit" friends, I felt peripheral, barely included. Sadness and shame weighed me down, visible in my hunched shoulders, my downcast head, my fringe covering my face. I wore oversized jumpers, hiding myself like a Bilby—small, timid, always on alert.

I tried to break through. I approached people with fake courage, overcompensated with enthusiasm, but nothing worked. I remember racing to sit next to a popular girl in class, thrilled to claim the seat. She looked at me with disgust. The look pierced me deeper than words. My body folded inward, shame pressing me down.

There were mornings when the house felt like a stage set that had shifted overnight. The hall smelled of cleaning products and chalk, the tiles crisp underfoot, the clock on the wall ticking with a stubborn patience that mocked my impatience. I learned to keep a map of futures inside my head—calculations about when to laugh, when to whisper, when to disappear behind a corridor of lockers. My notebook carried the conversations I wished I could have, written in careful print, a place where I could pretend I mattered by being perfectly ordinary.

Moments like these attacked my identity. They told me I was not good enough, that inclusion was conditional, that my worth was measured by others' acceptance. Each rejection carved another groove into the belief that I was inadequate. Even in the shame, I kept trying—approaching people, showing up, refusing to disappear completely. That persistence was the seed of resilience, and yet it carried a complication: the more I tried to tune myself to belong, the more I learned to mistrust the noise of my own needs.

The body, again, was the witness. A shoulder blade that ached any time someone asked for more than I felt I could give. A throat that would tighten when a classmate laughed at a joke I didn't understand. A stomach that folded into itself on the bus, when the driver asked if I'd sit with the cheerleaders, because the seat next to them seemed like an invitation to a moral fall I wasn't ready to accept.

I kept a ledger of tiny rebellions, too: the day I wore a different hoodie to school, the day I chose to answer a question aloud without forcing a smile for approval, the moment I refused to clap when the crowd did. Those small refusals felt like survival rituals. They were a way to tell my own body and mind: you have a voice, even if it's often silenced outside the moment you feel safe enough to use it.

By thirteen, the fear of rejection was no longer a fear so much as a map. I learned to predict the weather of a room—the way the doors opened and the way a word could travel and vanish, the way a gesture could land as a blessing or a wound. The more I learned the rules, the more I learned how to bend, pause, and retreat without burning bridges I couldn't bear to cross. I did not master belonging, but I learned how to borrow belonging from the moment when the room allowed me to exist without apology.

Despite the ache, I found stubborn pockets of companionship—people who saw me when I didn't see myself. Misfit circles, quiet corners of a library, a friend who shared a pencil and a story about a character who finally claimed a voice. These were the threads that began stitching themselves into a different fabric of self-worth, one that learned to value presence over perfection, honesty over performance, and tenderness over sheer protection.

Reflection

These formative incidents shaped the core of my self-worth. Abuse at seven taught me that vulnerability was dangerous. Dismissal at the bonfire taught me that grief could be inconvenient. Schoolyard rejection taught me that inclusion was conditional.

My body carried these lessons forward—clenched fists, hunched shoulders, shallow breaths, oversized jumpers hiding who I was. I internalised the belief that I was inadequate, unworthy, invisible. My spine carried the weight of a thousand small disappointments, each one a pinhole widening the channel through which self-doubt flowed. It was as if the body became an archive, storing each disappointment like a ghost at the back of the throat. My legs memorised the way fear could travel from hip to knee to ankle, a tremor that would sometimes shudder through me at a grocery-store line or the click of a door unlocking at dusk.

And yet, beneath the shame, there was always a flicker of hope. A stubborn seed that whispered: there is something good in me. That seed was a melody threaded through the noise — notes of ache and notes of resilience entwined. It kept me trying, kept me bending over backwards for others, kept me searching for connection even when rejection seemed inevitable. It was the same seed that later made me susceptible to manipulation—the hope that if I tried harder, proved myself more, someone would finally see me, value me, love me.

The "if I try harder" impulse was not a lack of intelligence or strength alone; it was a body's memory of a world that often spoke in syllables of scarcity. If I could just be more compliant, if I could calibrate my voice to be more pleasing, if I could stop the tremor in my hands long enough to offer a breathless, perfect smile, then perhaps I would be protected. The logic felt sound in the moment, even as the emotional consequence bore down. It taught me about boundaries that were permeable, about love that came with a price tag, and about care that shifted shape depending on who was paying.

In the years since, I have learned another language for self-worth—a language that does not erase the parts that hurt but invites them to speak alongside the parts that heal. I have learned to track the body's memory not as a weapon but as a guide. When heat rises in my chest in a crowded room, I name it: this is the body remembering. When the throat tightens at the sight of a familiar face, I name it: this is fear and history leaning into the present moment to test the boundary between then and now. When the shoulders lift toward the ears at a moment of conflict, I name it: this is the posture of a person who has learned to survive by becoming smaller. And then I release: I am choosing to unlearn those postures, even if the mind and muscle remember them.

I have found places where self-worth can rest not on the approval of others but on the simple constancy of being seen by someone who can hold truth with care. A therapist's room that becomes a harbour; a friend's call that arrives with no agenda but listening; the moment in a quiet kitchen where a cup of tea cools and a speaker finds a voice that had long been waiting for recognition. These are the fragments that begin to outnumber the old ones, and with their accumulation, a new frame emerges—a frame in which vulnerability does not erase value but adds it, a frame in which honesty does not invite annihilation but invites connection.

The memory remains, of course. It sits in the corner of the room like a patient witness that won't disappear. It is a body-memory that can still blip in the centre of a crowded street, or surface in a familiar lullaby drifting through a late-night window. But the memory no longer commands the room with its full authority. It has a partner now—the memory of strength, the memory of choosing what to own and how to speak it aloud. The old fear is still there, a ghost at the back of the throat, but it's no longer the primary guest. The primary guest is the tenderness that grew despite it, the stubborn belief that I am not only what happened to me but what I choose to become because of it.

I carry the late afternoon of the teacup, the flame of the bonfire, the echo of school bells, as parts of a longer itinerary—the itinerary of a life that keeps arriving at the edge of a truth and choosing to stay. The body, which learned to extinguish, now learns to illuminate. It holds space for memory without becoming its prisoner. It allows tears to fall without dissolving the person who must keep moving. It teaches me that self-worth is not a single verdict but a slow, patient composition—notes of ache and notes of resilience entwined, a melody that does not pretend the pain did not happen but insists that the pain will not dictate the final measure.

I am not finished rewriting the map. The story is still expanding, still inviting new rooms to be opened—rooms where the self can see itself clearly without the fanfare of perfection. There are days when the old scripts still print themselves onto my skin, when a familiar reflex makes me shrink in a crowded room or swallow a word I want to say. And there are days when I can choose differently. To speak up. To tell the truth not as a demand for validation but as an act of self-respect. To move toward the people who can meet me at the table as I am, not as I was expected to be. The work remains tender and raw, a cinematic montage of childhood scenes repurposed by adulthood into something like grace.

If there is a refrain to these memories, it is this: the self is not born from the absence of harm but from the decision to bear it, to name it, to let it cohabitate with courage. The memory of a seven-year-old body silenced by fear does not need to own the entire script of my life any longer. For every memory that whispers, I am not enough, there is a breath that answers, I am still here. For every moment that pain trained me to hide, there is a moment that courage trained me to step forward and say: I belong to my own story. It is not a perfect story, and it will not erase what happened, but it is mine to tell, mine to heal, mine to grow from.

And so I keep listening to the tender, raw music of memory, letting body and voice legibly translate the ache into something that can be lived with—carefully, honestly, beautifully. The vignettes are not simply relics; they are instruments. The cup of tea, the bonfire, the schoolyard—each is a drumbeat inside my chest, a reminder that even in the deepest quiet, the body remembers, and the memory, in turn, can become a way forward. The self-worth I am stitching together is not about pretending the wounds did not happen but about naming them with mercy and choosing, every day, to keep going even when a part of me wants to retreat. It is enough that I show up to the page, to the room, to the room within myself where the truth can breathe, where tenderness and truth can coexist, where I can finally let the memory be a teacher rather than a tyrant.

And perhaps that is the final line of this film—the body as archive, memory as witness, and the self as a stubborn, ongoing reconstruction. I am still here. I am building a life where a seven-year-old's fear of not mattering does not determine my capacity to matter today. I am teaching myself to hold two truths. The past is heavy, and I can carry it with care. Form rises from fragments into a shape large enough to cradle both harm and possibility. That is how form becomes form—the ascent from fragments to a shape large enough to cradle both what happened and what is possible beyond it. It is a tenderness, a rawness, and a cinematic quiet that brews in the kitchen of a memory, turning chaos into a language I can finally speak aloud.

Reflection — The Body Speaks When Words Cannot

Introduction: The Language of Pain

Reflection is not merely memory; it is the body's archive. Every ache, every cramp, every shiver is a note in a diary my mind often cannot read. Childhood rehearsed silence, but my body never stopped speaking. It spoke in ways adults dismissed, in ways teachers misunderstood, in ways peers ignored. Pain bent me inward, cramps curled me into protective shapes, and stomach aches became the vocabulary I lacked — the words I could not say aloud. Each spasm was a signal: unsafe. Each twist of the gut was a warning: proceed with caution. My body carried these messages before my mind had the language to comprehend them.

Those early communications were rehearsals for survival. And while they brought shame, discomfort, and exhaustion, they were also proof — proof that my body had an innate intelligence, a wisdom, a capacity to protect me when words were insufficient.

Vignette 1: The Weight of Mornings

Every morning before high school carried weight heavier than my schoolbag. It wasn't simply the academic expectations, the homework, or the fear of embarrassment — it was a premonition embedded in my body. My stomach clenched, knots coiling tight before I even put my shoes on. The heaviness wasn't metaphorical; it was visceral, pressing down on my diaphragm, making breathing feel deliberate and difficult.

Walking to the gates became a negotiation with the architecture of my body. Shoulders hunched, breath shallow, eyes fixed on the cracks in the pavement — each step was calculated, a rehearsal of invisibility. My body anticipated humiliation, confrontation, exclusion, and physical threat long before my mind could even frame them as possible. I learned that survival wasn't about courage. It was about being small. Invisible. Unremarkable.

The walk to school became a ritual of containment. Each muscle engaged in restraint, each thought whispered, *don't draw attention, don't get hurt.* By the time I reached the gates, I was drained, not from effort, but from anticipation — my body having already processed the danger before the day even began.

Vignette 2: The Payphone

Year nine. The pain bent me in half, sharp and relentless, echoing across my stomach and chest like a warning drum. My brown jumper hung heavy on my frame, absorbing my tension as I shuffled past empty classrooms, past the woodwork and metalwork rooms, past the oval where kids laughed and played T-ball. Each step was a plea for survival, a prayer that I could reach the gym without incident. My body was a compass pointing to danger, its signals too loud to ignore.

The double doors opened into a rush of cold air, the kind that always lived in the lower levels of the school. I leaned into it, letting the chill wash over me, craving relief. The orange payphone waited like a lifeline. My hands shook as I lifted the handset and, through trembling fingers, gave the operator Mum's number. Relief arrived with her voice — warm, familiar, safe. My muscles loosened, my chest unclenched, the world momentarily righted itself. Fifteen minutes later, her car rounded the corner, and the tension released like a tide retreating.

The next day came with the same ritual. The same preemptive fear, the same body-language of caution. What I could not articulate with words — my dread, my sense of exposure, my longing for safety — my body broadcasted clearly to anyone paying attention. It was a vocabulary of survival, a language of pain that accompanied me throughout adolescence.

Vignette 3: The Sleepover

After the abuse at seven, the world of sleepovers became a minefield. I longed to belong, to experience friendship as unburdened children do. I liked her — my friend — and wanted to stay overnight. Yet fear pressed in like a physical weight, curling tight in my stomach and coiling my intestines into warning signals. I clutched my belly, each twist and spasm a message I could not translate into words: *I am not safe.*

"I have a tummy ache," I whispered, voice small and urgent. Relief came with the familiar footsteps of Mum, fetching me home. The shame of leaving early was palpable, a knot that wound itself tight around my chest. Yet the relief of escape — the return to safety — was stronger. My body had spoken for me, louder than my mouth ever could. It had communicated need, fear, and a request for protection, all without articulation. This was a lesson that would echo in my life: sometimes survival requires a language older than words, and the body knows what the mind cannot yet comprehend.

Vignette 4: The Brownies Hall

Another night, another attempt at belonging. Brownies had organised a sleep-over at the community hall, a cavernous space that smelled faintly of dust and varnish. I wasn't excited. Mum had been a Girl Guide, and I was expected to follow suit. Participation was non-negotiable. Yet as the night stretched on, un-ease grew. Shadows pressed against the walls, and every creak of the floorboard amplified my anxiety.

My stomach cramped again, sharp and insistent. The familiar twist of tension — a primal warning — spoke more clearly than my protestations ever could. I whispered about my tummy ache, and once again, Mum came to fetch me. Maybe I truly was ill, or maybe my body was telling the truth I could not speak aloud: *I do not feel safe here.*

In those moments, the distinction between illness and instinct blurred. Pain be-came a guide, a messenger, a subtle scream of survival. My body had been hon-ing its capacity to communicate since childhood, and now it performed with precision, even when the world around me misunderstood its signals.

Vignette 5: The Locker

Year seven. Part of a group, yet always on the bottom rung, I navigated the so-cial hierarchies with caution. The most confident girl — with her triangular hair that fanned outward like a weapon — held power over the small ecosystem of the locker bay. She had her followers, a silent army ready to enforce her whims. If I dared to oppose her, the consequences were swift, public, and hu-miliating.

Her locker was close to mine. I had a combination lock, a fragile sense of con-trol in a world that often felt unpredictable. Somehow, she discovered the code. She took the lock. The bell had already rung, and panic surged through me like electricity. I needed my books. I needed to be the good girl who followed rules. I asked, begged, and pleaded for the lock back. She laughed, her amusement piercing, each giggle a reminder of my invisibility. No one intervened. No one helped.

Panic escalated until my body betrayed me. In a flash of shame, desperation, and instinct, I grabbed her hand and tried to bite it. She recoiled before it landed.

The damage, however, was done. She made a spectacle of me, amplifying my humiliation, and the familiar language of my body screamed louder than ever: *I am unsafe. I am unseen. I am unheard.*

Years later, I saw her again on a train. Triangular hair, same tracksuit pants. The confidence had dulled, life having altered her trajectory. But I did not dwell on her changes. What remained vivid was the memory of my own body sounding alarms — the first messenger of danger, of betrayal, of survival. That memory would follow me long into adulthood, informing how I navigated relationships, authority, and the spaces in between.

Reflection Vignette — The Country School

Not all memories of childhood were shadowed. My first three years were spent at a tiny country school of about a hundred students. It had a warmth that wrapped around me, a friendliness mixed with the crisp, sweet smell of pine trees lining the borders. Play was communal. Games like one free home brought the entire school together, bigger kids shepherding the littler ones, teaching rules, enforcing fairness, protecting the young in the chaos.

I remember the thrill of running across the yard, lungs burning, laughter spilling uncontrollably, the ground alive beneath my shoes. When the asphalt court arrived, it became the stage for British Bulldogs. Rough, loud, competitive, and yet inclusive. My body remembers the adrenaline, the pounding of feet, the laughter, the collective joy of belonging. There were moments of unguarded connection, where I felt held by community and tethered to safety not dictated by fear but by mutual engagement.

These memories are tender because they remind me: my body is not only a warning system. It is also a vessel for joy, for connection, for exhilaration. It remembers the taste of freedom, the thrill of being held by collective play, and the electric pulse of belonging. Even in the presence of trauma, my body retains the capacity to know delight.

Reflection: The Body's Archive

Looking back, I see how my body carried the weight of what I could not articulate. Abdominal pain, cramps, tightening, and somatic tension became a lexicon of loneliness, fear, and dismissal. Each ache was a message: *You are not safe. You are not seen. You are not heard.*

This archive was rehearsed in childhood and repeated through adolescence. Every payphone call, every fabricated tummy ache, every protective tensing in social settings was an act of survival. These signals influenced my adult relationships, making me susceptible to manipulation and tethering me to patterns where my voice could be silenced. My body's wisdom became my first and sometimes only guide.

Yet within that pain lay resilience. Every tremor, every twist, every flare of discomfort was proof of a system that had not abandoned me. It warned me. Protected me. Guided me. Pain was survival encoded in muscle memory.

The body does not lie. The stomach tightens when we sense threat, the chest constricts when we anticipate danger, the hands tremble when we are overwhelmed. These are not weaknesses — they are ancient signals that our survival matters.

Closing: The Cost and the Gift

Reflection illuminates both cost and gift. Pain was the choreography of survival, rehearsed in childhood, performed through adolescence, carried into adulthood. Every vignette — the payphone, the sleepover, the locker — was a rehearsal for future vulnerabilities, foreshadowing the rejection and manipulation that would come. Each flare was training for the world, each ache a silent mentor.

Yet pain was also a gift. It was the body speaking when words failed. It told me when I was unsafe, unseen, unheard. It guided me to protection when the world offered none. It refused to abandon me.

Tender and raw, these memories testify to the resilience embedded in the human body. Listening to these signals reveals the possibility of healing — the chance to reclaim self-worth, not from the recognition of others, but from the innate wisdom of the body itself. Survival is not weakness. It is strength, intelligence, and the doorway to compassionate healing.

Foreshadowing — The Misfits and the Threshold of Adulthood

By the time I reached Year 10, the early blueprints of childhood had already shaped me in ways I would not understand until much later. Every lesson, every silent rule, every subtle cue from adults and peers had been encoded into my nervous system. I carried unspoken instructions like choreography, muscle memory performing them before thought: shrink, comply, endure, absorb. These movements were rehearsed in the body long before they reached conscious awareness.

It was during this period that I gravitated toward the misfits, the kids who smoked at the back of the school. I wasn't a smoker — never touched one — yet I lingered there, hovering at the edge, fascinated by the audacity of their world. They exhaled smoke like currency, like they held some secret to the universe that the rest of us hadn't yet discovered. I didn't inhale. I simply observed, listened, and learned. I held their jokes, their secrets, their defiance. I felt the tug of belonging like a physical pull in my chest, a warmth that was slightly illicit, almost dangerous.

My body remembers it vividly: the shallow, rapid breaths of trying to appear nonchalant, the jaw clenched to hide the nervousness, the folded shoulders making me smaller, as if invisibility was a costume that might shield me from judgment. The space behind the school became my early training ground — a laboratory for human interaction, negotiation, and camouflage. I was learning how to bend myself to match the energy of a group, to adjust tone, posture, and presence just enough to be tolerated. Little did I know, this pattern would echo through every relationship and social situation in my adulthood.

Vignette: Sliding Grades

My grades began to slide long before anyone noticed. At first, it was imperceptible: one missed homework assignment, a test not studied for, a report handed in late. Each small misstep quietly chipped away at my fragile sense of worth. What once defined me — the marks on the page, the validation from teachers, the recognition that I was "good at school" — began to slip like sand through my fingers.

Schoolwork became secondary to connection. The phone calls after class, the laughter spilling across the corded handset, the thrill of being part of something alive, chaotic, unstructured — these mattered more than neat assignments or good marks. My body carried the tension of these divided loyalties. Cramps twisted through my stomach at the thought of failing, panic surged in my bloodstream when teachers asked for overdue work, and shallow breaths reminded me constantly of the impossible balancing act I was performing.

I told myself it didn't matter. I told myself I was just doing what everyone else was doing. But deep in my chest, a quieter truth pulsed: I didn't want to disappoint anyone — not my teachers, not my family, not my friends. I was learning to prioritise external approval over my own goals, to value connection above competence. This lesson, subtle at the time, would later make manipulation feel familiar, almost natural. My nervous system had been trained to bend to preserve closeness.

Vignette: Year 12 Results

By Year 12, the slide had momentum. I passed my exams, but the shame that followed was immediate and visceral. I remember folding the results quickly, as if hiding them might erase the truth. My cheeks burned with heat, my chest felt tight, and my breath caught just below my throat.

The shame wasn't truly about academics. It was about identity. It taught me to carry inadequacy quietly, to internalise disappointment as a flaw within myself rather than a temporary circumstance. I didn't share my feelings — not because I didn't want support, but because I had learned, through years of observation and experience, to be a buffer between my truth and the outside world.

That moment carved a lasting instruction into my psyche: don't take up space. Don't reveal too much. Don't let the world see where you feel small. Shame became a silent companion, whispering that vulnerability was dangerous. Years later, when partners twisted my uncertainty into leverage or weaponised my self-doubt, compliance felt almost instinctive. Not because I lacked strength, but because I had been conditioned to protect myself through acquiescence long before adulthood arrived.

Vignette: TAFE and Abandonment

After school, I enrolled in a secretary course at TAFE. I made it three-quarters of the way before quitting. I remember the fluorescent-lit rooms, the smell of paperwork and polished linoleum, the oppressive hum of fluorescent tubes overhead. My body remembers the experience more vividly than my conscious mind: the tension in my shoulders every time someone corrected me, the constriction in my throat when instructions felt like judgment, the subtle panic rising whenever authority approached.

I had just turned eighteen — legally an adult, newly free — yet the walls of expectation felt suffocating. I wanted out. I wanted to be with friends, to belong, to be included in spaces where I felt seen. Connection outweighed structure; belonging eclipsed completion.

The course was abandoned, but the lesson remained. My susceptibility lay not in failure but in hunger — the hunger to be chosen, to be welcomed, to be safe in social bonds. I learned that I would rather disappoint myself than someone else. That pattern — loyalty to connection above self-preservation — would later become fertile ground for manipulation. Not because of weakness, but because my nervous system had been primed to prioritise relational closeness over self-protection.

Vignette: Nights Out

I wasn't a big drinker, but I loved being the designated driver. It gave me a sense of control, of purpose, of being essential. Driving became a metaphorical anchor, a role that allowed me to belong without surrendering myself. The car was my sanctuary, a space where I could navigate chaos safely.

I remember the freedom of the open road, the highway lit only by street-lamps, the adrenaline of late nights punctuated by laughter and music. For the first time, I felt a sense of competence and authority over my environment. I wasn't reckless; I was dependable. I wasn't wild; I was trusted.

Even in that role, the seeds of hyper-responsibility were planted. Being the driver meant staying sober so others could indulge. It meant watching, waiting, anticipating. It meant absorbing the unpredictability of others while maintaining calm. My nervous system learned a rhythm of hyper-vigilance, a preemptive awareness of potential danger, a careful calibration of energy to accommodate the moods and needs of those around me. This same pattern would later manifest in adulthood as walking on eggshells, smoothing conflicts, predicting emotional responses, and constantly managing relational dynamics. Childhood scripted the role; adolescence refined it. Adulthood simply carried it forward.

Reflection: The Threshold of Adulthood

At eighteen, I believed I was stepping into freedom. In truth, I was stepping into an echo. Every choice — friendship, risk, retreat — was guided by patterns etched long before adulthood arrived. Childhood had created templates for the roles I would play: the accommodator, the peacekeeper, the forgiver, the one who "understands" more than is fair.

The misfits behind the school, the sliding grades, the hidden results, the abandoned course, the late-night drives — they weren't isolated experiences. They were chapters of an origin story I hadn't yet realised I was writing. Each event carried lessons in body intelligence, early calibrations of safety and danger, early scripts of loyalty and compliance. My body remembered all of it: the stomach cramps of guilt, the shallow breaths of longing to belong, the folded shoulders of shame, the quiet endurance of invisibility.

These signals were not random. They were survival mechanisms. They marked where I was safe, where I was at risk, and where I needed to navigate with caution. I just didn't yet know how to read them consciously.

Vignette: Summer Jobs and Micro-Choices

The pattern of prioritising others above self became even more evident in summer jobs. I worked at a local café, constantly aware of colleagues' moods, the flow of orders, the customer's tone. My body learned to anticipate conflict, to absorb irritations without reacting, to bend to expectation quietly.

I recall one evening, juggling trays, struggling to remember an order, while a supervisor snapped at me for a minor delay. My chest tightened, stomach clenched, and every instinct whispered compliance. I said nothing, apologised excessively, and doubled my efforts. My mind catalogued failure, but my body encoded vigilance. The nervous system didn't forget.

This hyper-attunement, initially adaptive, became a template for adulthood. It taught me that if I moved smoothly enough, anticipated needs, and sacrificed my own comfort, I might escape criticism, disapproval, or rejection. It was an early blueprint for survival in both work and relational contexts.

Reflection: Seeds Blooming

Foreshadowing isn't prophecy; it's pattern recognition. Childhood had scripted silence, compliance, invisibility, and dependency into my nervous system. By eighteen, these seeds had begun to bloom. The misfits taught me the thrill and cost of belonging. Sliding grades taught me the tension between approval and competence. Hidden results taught me quiet endurance of shame. Abandoned courses and nights out taught me the visceral pull of connection over self-preservation.

These patterns didn't vanish in adulthood — they magnified. They shaped relationships where my voice could be manipulated, fears exploited, and loyalty leveraged. Not because I was weak, but because my nervous system had been primed to seek closeness at any cost.

Yet within these memories lies illumination. They reveal where I had been conditioned, where my nervous system had adapted for survival, and where awareness can create a path forward. Understanding the choreography of my body and history provides a map out of reactive patterns. It allows me to recognise the moment I am called to recalibrate — to prioritise safety, self-worth, and authenticity above the impulse to conform.

Adulthood did not erase childhood. It amplified it. It made patterns bigger, lessons louder, and vulnerabilities more visible. The danger, the manipulation, and the slow erosion of self that followed were not random — they were foreshadowed, rehearsed, and primed in the early years. Awareness of this origin story is not just insight; it is power. It is the first step in rewriting the chore-ography, in reclaiming agency, in transforming survival instinct into conscious presence.

By looking back, I see the map. I see the patterns, the body's archive, the seeds planted in adolescence that would later reveal the terrain of vulnerability and resilience. And in that map lies the potential to step forward differently — with awareness, boundaries, and the courage to value myself above the compulsion to belong.

I am still here, carrying both the scars and the strength, rewriting the choreog-raphy into my own.

Chapter 2: The Seduction & the Mask

The thrill of these nights had its own rhythm — one my body recognised long before my mind could articulate it. We spent the late afternoon in a flurry of preparations, the large bedroom alive with laughter, chatter, and the faint, sweet scent of cheap perfume. My friends and I swapped clothes, tried on each other's tops and skirts, fussed with our hair and makeup, teasing and critiquing in equal measure. The ritual felt almost sacred, a gateway into the night we were about to claim. We favoured edgy textures and bold colours that caught the dim lights in a way that made us feel seen but not overexposed. Every choice mattered. Every accessory, every swipe of mascara, every twist of hair was part of a performance we had perfected for these nights.

The energy of the ritual was contagious. There was something about the way we transformed ourselves together — the shared mirror, the borrowed eyeliner, the laughter that spilled across the room like champagne bubbles. We weren't just dressing; we were trying to wear confidence like a second skin. Each outfit was a declaration, each hairstyle a negotiation between individuality and group identity. My body buzzed with anticipation, the nervous energy of adolescence colliding with the thrill of stepping into adulthood. I didn't yet know that these rituals — the careful calibration of appearance, the hunger for validation — were foreshadowing deeper patterns that would later shape my relationships.

By the time we left, the town was a dim blur of streetlights and headlights, the air thick with the promise of chaos. The first club we hit was packed, pulsing with bass and bodies, girls on podiums swaying to the music, guys leaning against the bar or tossing darts of attention across the dance floor. We didn't have much money, but it didn't matter. Water was enough, and I was usually the designated driver anyway, though tonight I was free from that responsibility. We danced, we laughed, we moved as one entity, hungry for the night, hungry for the feeling of being alive.

The bass thudded through my chest — less music, more a second heartbeat. Lights strobing, faces flashing red, blue, gold. Smoke, sweat, perfume, spilled beer — a cocktail clinging to skin and fabric. My calves ached, heat climbed, and my body buzzed with the thrill of being anonymous in a room where everyone was both seen and unseen. Suspended in that moment, the night felt ordinary and extraordinary all at once — like countless others, yet entirely singular.

It was at this first club that my friend spotted him. Ex. He wasn't on the dance floor; he and his friends were huddled around a table, the smoke curling from their cigarettes in lazy spirals. There was a confidence about them, a rough-edged camaraderie that drew attention without asking for it. My friend nudged me, gesturing discreetly, and we drifted over.

We exchanged hellos, casual and easy, and I remember a faint thrill in my chest — not attraction, but the magnetic pull of being noticed. His presence was heavy, controlled, intense, and it sparked something I hadn't yet understood: the thrill of attention, the way someone could notice you and make you feel, however fleetingly, that your presence mattered. There were no grand gestures, no charm offensive, just a quiet, steady awareness that drew my focus.

I didn't yet understand the choreography my body was performing. The shallow breath, the tightened jaw, the folded shoulders — all of it was muscle memory from years of learning how to survive in spaces where belonging was conditional. My nervous system was already attuned to cues, reading subtle signals faster than my mind could interpret them. Ex's presence triggered a paradoxical rush: the thrill of being noticed, the tension of navigating someone unpredictable.

As the first club wound down at three in the morning, we piled into cars, a motley caravan of youthful energy, and headed to the next club twenty minutes away. It was still alive with music, the smell of spilled beer and cigarettes mingling with the synthetic pulse of neon lights. Pool tables lined one side, and for a moment, I lost myself in the clatter of cues and the easy laughter of my friends. But then his presence returned, Ex and his mates moving across the room, and I noticed a subtle shift. The guys we had been playing pool with dispersed, their energy retreating as if our small corner of the world had been claimed.

He had a rough, intimidating air, the kind that made others hesitant, respectful, or cautious. I wasn't used to that. My family had always been proper, measured, almost idyllic, like a Brady Bunch performing the perfect scene. This family — the one I was observing — was starkly different: raw, loud, chaotic. And there was something compelling about it. Not him personally, but the way his world operated, the tension and attention it commanded. It made my chest tighten in a way that was both thrilling and unnerving.

I remember one night vividly — he sensed a fight brewing with his brother, a tension that was about to snap into violence. He pulled me aside, eyes sharp, and without saying much, we left. The air outside the club was cool against my skin, but inside me, adrenaline coursed like wildfire. The next day, I heard that members of his family had been arrested, a violent fallout from the night. It should have frightened me, but instead, it etched a peculiar sense of awe into my memory: a world of chaos, controlled by a few, and the rush of being in its orbit.

Driving with him was another layer of thrill, reckless and intoxicating. I remember one drive in particular — his foot heavy on the accelerator, wind pushing my hair back, my body pressed against the car, the world blurring past. The speed was erratic and dangerous, and none of it impressed me — it just slammed adrenaline through my body, the kind that makes your nerves spark like faulty wiring.

The first nights with Ex blurred into chaos and allure. Casual club encounters spilled into streets, cars, and the unpredictable pulse of his world. I had grown up in a family where order was prized — routines, politeness, measured tones. With him, everything was raw, unfiltered, and alive. My body, already trained to sense danger, misread volatility as significance. It was as if my nervous system whispered: this feels familiar, therefore it must be important.

Travelling together was its own initiation. His foot pressed hard on the accelerator, the car surging forward like a beast straining against its leash. Streetlights blurred into golden streaks, each one flashing across the windshield like a warning I couldn't quite decipher. Speed rattled my bones, pressed me against the door, hair whipping across my face. My chest tightened from fear — I'd grown up fastening seatbelts, obeying rules, measuring risk. Here, chaos ruled, and my body drank the low-level cortisol.

One night, the drive was so fast the world tilted sideways. My head bounced lightly against the glass, tires roaring like an unrestrained beast. I told him to slow down, but he didn't listen. Panic coiled in my chest, and instinct took over — I hit him, desperate, hard, thinking it might force control. But the more I struck, the faster he drove, adrenaline and recklessness doubling with every blow. My breaths came shallow and sharp, a frantic rhythm I couldn't steady, and I realised fear wasn't part of the thrill — it was the engine itself.

Later, I realised how deeply those drives etched themselves into my nervous system. It wasn't the adrenaline that drew me in — it was the illusion of significance, the small, sharp comfort of being noticed, of attention directed at me. My body learned to equate risk with presence, chaos with importance. It was a rehearsal for the years ahead, where volatility would masquerade as intimacy, and vigilance would become my default posture.

There were quieter moments too, pockets of normalcy that felt almost tender. Nights spent playing PlayStation — racing games, Abe's Odyssey — where competition replaced conversation. His focus on the screen was intense, but contained. I clung to those moments as if they were islands of stability. In the games, he was predictable: win, lose, restart. In life, he was anything but. My body relaxed slightly in those hours, the tension in my shoulders easing, the rhythm of fear temporarily suspended.

Yet even in those pockets, the undercurrent remained. A glance too long at another guy, a laugh shared with his brother, could spark jealousy. His jaw tightened, his eyes narrowed, and the air shifted. I learned to moderate my behaviour, to shrink my attention, to avoid interactions that might trigger the storm. My body remembered the early lessons of schoolyard survival: tight chest, shallow breath, folded shoulders. Compliance became second nature.

Looking back, I see how my childhood primed me for these moments. My father's anger, my grandfather's unpredictability — they had already taught me to anticipate moods, to silence dissent, to survive through vigilance. Rationalisation became my shield: he's young, we're young, anger is normal. Fear was not foreign; it was familiar, a language I understood well. My nervous system had been rehearsing this dance for years, and now it found fertile ground in intimacy.

What drew me in wasn't him personally, but the thrill of attention, the contrast with my own upbringing. My family had been proper, measured, almost idyllic. His world was loud, unbound by rules, unfiltered. It was intoxicating to step into that rawness, to feel the pull of someone who commanded notice without asking. My chest tightened with the electric thrill of being seen, mistaking attention for significance. I didn't yet understand that the same qualities that had shielded me from external chaos could later be turned inward, weaponised against me.

These early encounters — the reckless drives, the video games, the subtle cues of control — were not isolated experiences. My body was learning, encoding, adapting. The shallow breath, the clenched jaw, the tensed shoulders — all of it was muscle memory carried forward from adolescence. What felt like thrill was foreshadowing. What felt like belonging was rehearsal. And what felt like intimacy was, in truth, the body's archive of survival, replayed in a new theatre.

The townhouse was small, dimly lit, carrying the faint scent of incense, old carpets and stale cigarette smoke. It wasn't the kind of place you imagined moving into when dreaming of adulthood. The fridge was tiny, the couch and dining table came as a package deal, and the bed creaked with every shift. My parents had bought us a washing machine—a practical gesture. Even in disorder, fragments of normal life tried to hold their ground.

Every morning, light filtered through the pull-down blind, mingling with the lingering smoke that clung stubbornly to curtains and clothes. I lay still, listening for cues—the rhythm of his breathing, the shuffle of his footsteps, the tone of his first words. My body, trained from childhood, measured the energy of the room before my mind had even opened its eyes. Safety was never guaranteed; it had to be negotiated, moment by moment.

Ex's anger was noticeable, though not constant. It arrived like a storm front—sudden and unpredictable. A word, a glance, a tone could shift the air. His drug use—bongs, cigarettes, alcohol—hovered like a fog, dulling some edges while sharpening others. I didn't touch any of it; I couldn't.

I began noticing the rhythm of the cycle. Panic coiled in his chest the moment he ran low on smoke or cigarettes, jittery anxiety building until he obtained more. Trips out—to his mates' houses, anywhere he could get it. If the money wasn't there, or drinks were mixed, tension snapped. The anger leaked slowly at first, then sharply, cutting through the room like a sudden gust. My body, trained to anticipate, tightened and braced, counting the beats between craving, frustration, and eruption. His habits set the rhythm of our lives, dictating moods, conversations, silences. My nervous system catalogued each shift, rehearsing vigilance as though it were a daily ritual.

Evenings sometimes offered brief pockets of normalcy—games, competition, islands of stability. In the games, he was focused, competitive, contained. In life, he was volatile, erratic, and often unreachable. My body relaxed slightly in those hours; shoulders eased, breath deepened—but the reprieve was temporary. The tension always returned, like a tide that refused to recede.

Family visits added another layer of chaos. His brother often stayed with us—unkempt, abrasive, rude to my parents. One visit erupted into confrontation in front of them. Voices rose, walls were kicked, the air thick with aggression. I stood to the side, heart hammering, unsure whether to intervene or retreat. My parents' unease was palpable; their polite attempts at civility collapsed under the weight of volatility. I tried to mediate, smooth over, maintain fragile peace, but fractures were evident. The townhouse became a crucible, its walls scarred witnesses to a dynamic equal parts seduction and intimidation.

Concern etched itself onto my parents' faces—the worry in their tone, the way their eyes searched mine for a sign I would come with them. They didn't want to leave me there—their meek daughter, beside a bikie-like figure who had just had a run-in with his brother. But I refused. I couldn't walk away. Ex made me feel special, wanted, chosen in a way I had never felt before. Their concern collided with my craving for recognition, and in that collision, I chose him. The decision was not logical; it was visceral. My body leaned toward belonging, even as my parents' voices tried to anchor me back to safety.

I can't overstate the rush of being wanted—chosen. It was intoxicating, oxygen after years of holding my breath. My parents worked seven days a week, their lives consumed by duty and survival. My brother was the favourite, celebrated, cherished. I was the quiet one, the compliant one—the daughter who learned early that invisibility was safer than disappointment. So when Ex looked at me, pulled me into his orbit, it felt like proof that I mattered. His anger didn't frighten me at first—it felt normal, familiar, almost expected. Attention was the currency I craved; I mistook its volatility for care. My body buzzed with the thrill of being wanted, even as my nervous system whispered warnings I couldn't yet translate.

Domestic routines carried their own storms. Cooking, folding laundry, washing dishes—each task shadowed by the question of mood. Would silence stretch into hours? Would irritation flare into anger? Would tenderness arrive unexpectedly, a rare gift? My body rehearsed responses: shallow breath when tension rose, clenched jaw when silence thickened, tensed shoulders when anger simmered. Compliance became skill, attentiveness a necessity, emotional restraint a shield.

Intimacy was complicated. Early encounters had already taught me the difference between consent and expectation. Pain in my belly, discomfort voiced but ignored, boundaries blurred. His persistence, coupled with rare moments of tenderness, created a confusing mix of care and control. My body learned to signal distress without words—a silent language of tension, withdrawal, anticipatory anxiety. I thought physical connection would bridge emotional gaps, but it only highlighted imbalance: my voice, comfort, pleasure—secondary, negotiable.

He came to pick me up at the train station after work, his goatee freshly shaved. Beneath the rough exterior, he looked... impossibly alluring. I couldn't believe someone like him could be interested in me. It was intoxicating, like winning a lottery I hadn't bought a ticket for. Yet beneath every glance, every smile, the same pattern lingered—intensity, control, and an unspoken negotiation of safety I had learned to navigate long before him. He was sensitive in a way that demanded caution; one wrong word, one misplaced tone, and the smallest spark could ignite anger. I measured everything, careful not to provoke the storm beneath his gravitas.

Nights out followed predictable patterns. Friends' houses and family gatherings became stages for display and surveillance. I wasn't a heavy drinker; my role as designated driver kept me anchored, alert. Even in small freedoms, my body registered tension, scanning for cues hinting at danger, disappointment, or conflict. I was learning, once again, to navigate a world demanding constant attention—where allure masked control, and thrill shadowed risk.

Psychologically, my past mingled with the present. My father's anger, my grandfather's unpredictability, the early conditioning of silent compliance—all informed my responses. Rationalisation became necessary: this was youth, this was experience, this was life. Yet beneath it simmered unease. My nervous system, trained over decades, read cues long before my mind catalogued them. Fear wasn't foreign; it was familiar, a language I spoke fluently.

I grew up in what looked like a perfect household—orderly, proper. Beneath the veneer was a philosophy of obedience. The 80s and 90s were gold-star parenting years: "I've put a roof over your head, food in your belly, clothes on your back—that's enough." You didn't speak unless spoken to. You put others' needs ahead of your own. You respected elders regardless of treatment. Compliance was demanded, not just expected. These lessons taught me invisibility, that my voice didn't matter. Chase Hughes (leading expert in human behaviour, influence and persuasion) warns against raising children to be blindly obedient, particularly young girls, because natural inclination to respond to authority can be exploited. I was not taught that. I was taught to obey. That obedience became the soil in which manipulation could take root, priming me to tolerate anger, volatility, and control as rules of engagement.

Friendships and social interactions layered complexity into daily life. Ex's mates became my friends by default. They were extensions of his world, and I navigated them cautiously. Loyalty was expected, boundaries porous, social manoeuvring a second nature. Pool games, drugs, alcohol, music—arenas of connection and subtle negotiation. I learned to anticipate moods, manage proximity, exist without drawing attention, survive within his orbit.

As my world bent toward Ex, friendships thinned. I saw less of the girls who had once been anchors; their laughter replaced by raw chaos. It was during this time I had an abortion. I told one friend, desperate for someone to hold the weight of my secret. Years later, my mother revealed the friend had told her. Knowing she had known all along made me feel sick, carrying shame in silence while others whispered it aloud. I remembered the secrecy, the tightening in my chest, the nausea rising at the betrayal.

In retrospect, the townhouse was more than a place to live; it was a crucible. The magnetism, fleeting affection, and seduction layered over a foundation of control and unpredictability. Its walls absorbed volatility, its rooms witnessed the oscillation between tenderness and threat. My nervous system catalogued the push and pull, the highs and lows, every argument, silent treatment, flare of anger, playful tease, night of reckless driving—imprinted in muscle memory, shaping instincts that later governed decisions, relationships, survival. What felt like domestic life was, in truth, a training ground—where compliance became skill, vigilance instinct, and survival choreography became a blueprint I carried into adulthood.

Chapter 3: The Hidden Reality

When you've been gaslit enough times, you reach a point where your own words feel hollow, even when they come from one of your most sacred truths: honesty. I've always carried truth as a core value, a compass in a world that often asks you to bend. But when someone lies to you over and over, not just casually, but deliberately, it pierces deeper than betrayal—it strikes the very marrow of your conviction. You start to wonder if anyone would believe you, if anyone could, if your own perception is a trap.

There's a constant turning of events, a subtle, sinister rearrangement of reality where your actions, your intentions, even your words are contorted until they appear as faults of your own making. That is the architecture of gaslighting: small, repeated inversions that make you question the foundation of yourself.

I remember one clear moment with Mia, our daughter, though instances blur over the years. She had left home, beginning her own life, but she still reached out. Then one day, she told me she needed space. She cared for me, but she needed to protect herself and her boundaries to move forward. There was no malice in this, only survival, self-preservation. I understood and even felt grateful that she was prioritising her wellbeing.

When I returned home, I wanted to tell Ex what she had said, but I hesitated. Even sharing this truth felt like an act of cruelty. His presence was a silent judgment, a measuring of my loyalty to him over my own honesty. Months later, at an unexpected lunch with his brother, Mia's absence came up. I said she needed space. Ex froze for a moment and then leaned in, accusing: "Wait... you told me she didn't want to see you. So you lied to me."

That single phrase—"you lied"—became a weapon. I do not lie. Honesty is one of my top five values, unshakable. But what I had withheld was the truth of my choice: she didn't want contact because I had chosen to stay with him. My silence was never a lie, but in his framing, it was a betrayal, a manipulation, a confirmation that I was somehow untrustworthy. This wasn't a one-off. It became a recurring indictment, a means to destabilise my confidence in myself. That accusation was not isolated; it was part of a larger pattern where denial became his default language.

Gaslighting seeped into other areas too. Drugs. The constant denials. I could smell it, yet he would swear black and blue that he had not purchased or used anything. falsehoods spilled into moments that didn't even require them, saturating even the ordinary. Even when the truth was harmless. One day he said he was heading west into town. I later found he had veered east, guided by some hidden need to find his dealer. Money followed the same pattern—given freely, spent recklessly, withheld under threat, creating a constant tension that I navigated with quiet endurance.

Even small truths became battlefields. Giving him money for bills only to discover nothing had been paid. Taking it back over, reasserting control over a life that had already been hollowed by deceit. It was relentless, unyielding, and always tinged with the suggestion that I had failed, that my competence was a lie, that my perception was faulty.

This constant twisting of reality, the relentless undermining of my words, chipped away at my confidence. I began to measure everything I said, everything I did, against the potential of it being used against me. Truth became a precarious commodity, and I learned to navigate the terrain of fear, guilt, and manipulated doubt.

It was an erosion, gradual but profound, leaving a residue of hesitation, suspicion, and internal conflict. A subtle claustrophobia settled in—the sense that no statement, no gesture, no assertion of fact was free from reinterpretation, accusation, or betrayal. And all the while, my own moral compass, my own innate sense of right, was tested daily, sharpened against the jagged edges of his manipulations.

In the silence of that house, I became adept at parsing layers of falsehoods, recognising the patterns that threatened my mind, my truth. The cost was high: a life lived in hesitation, truth hollowed into suspicion, and the daily negotiation between authenticity and survival under a man who wielded lies not as slips of the tongue but as instruments of control.

Money became another battlefield. It wasn't just about dollars and cents—it was about survival, about safety, about a quiet, insidious assertion of control. I handled the household funds because someone had to ensure the bills were paid, the mortgage managed, the children clothed and fed. But even that responsibility was fraught with tension.

He could take fifty dollars and, by the time he returned, it would have vanished—spent on drugs, alcohol, cigarettes, or whim. I once entrusted him with the bills and the mortgage, only to discover later that nothing had been paid. I had to reclaim control, reconcile accounts, and restore order, all while holding down a part-time job, managing the children's schedules, picking them up and dropping them off, and somehow keeping the household afloat.

There were times when his full-time income, meant to sustain the family, disappeared entirely into substance use. Yet somehow, despite exhaustion and scarcity, I managed. We ate sausages more often than I can count. Pyjamas were never new-just old t-shirts and tracksuit pants, handed down, patched, repurposed. Newness, luxury, self-care—foreign concepts, sacrificed in the churn of survival.

Even gifts were rare, almost impossible. I never bought myself perfume; the one I've worn was given to me by my daughter, thoughtful, intentional, a bright fruity scent that affirmed me as a person, separate from the chaos.

Coercion was subtle but sharp. Requests for money came with an unspoken threat: the implication of anger, disappointment, or punishment if I refused. I always gave in. I had learned early that resistance carried risk. I would try to pull back, to budget, to safeguard what little remained. But every plan ran up against an invisible wall of manipulation.

Holidays, trips, even family gatherings became fraught exercises in control. Going away wasn't relief; it was another stage for power to play out. Cruises, safaris, overseas excursions—all shadowed by tension, threat, or neglect. On our wedding night, rather than sharing it with me, he spent time with two women I dubbed "the princesses," who only emerged after dark, carefully curated, glamorous, unreachable. I lay alone in the cabin, ill, ignored.

Even on trips meant for rest, he drifted away—smoking, drinking, chasing indulgence—while the family carried on without him. On an African safari, while I hand-washed clothes for the family, he frequented pubs and bars, joining people from the tour, ignoring responsibility, his presence an erratic shadow, as if the world revolved around the fulfillment of his cravings.

At every turn, the veneer of normalcy was punctured by aggression or subtle threats. A casual smirk, misinterpreted or weaponised, could provoke a violent response. At one campsite, a simple smile became ammunition-his threat to wipe that smirk from my face. Even my daughters mirrored these tensions, carrying echoes of discomfort from a father who calibrated violence to control.

Trips to Thailand, Cambodia, Africa—every excursion tested endurance. The heat was merciless, pressing down with a weight that felt almost physical. Forty degrees and climbing, the air thick enough to choke. I carried two litres of water, the bottle heavy in my hand, the only shield I had against the sun. A hat shaded my face, but I was the only one prepared. Ex, the couple with us-sluggish, irritated, exposed beneath the sun. No one seemed to want to be there. I did. Angkor Wat had always fascinated me, its stone towers rising like a mirage from centuries past.

But interest quickly became obligation. Their thirst grew, their discomfort sharpened, and I felt the silent demand to share. I offered my water, trying to ease the strain, but they drank without care, draining it as if it were endless. By the time we finished at the main temple and began the walk back to the tuk tuk, my bottle was nearly empty. I shielded myself from the sun, skin prickling, the undercurrent of threat already humming beneath the surface.

The journey continued, not toward relief but deeper into endurance. The trek to the temple where Angelina Jolie had filmed *Tomb Raider* was punishing. The tuk tuk strained against steep hills, forcing us out to walk, sweat soaking through clothes, legs burning, before climbing back in to continue. Each stop felt heavier, each climb more exhausting.

When we finally reached the last point, the driver told us we would need to walk another ten minutes to reach the temple. Ten minutes in that heat felt like an eternity. The couple refused, their faces set in frustration. Ex's mood shifted sharply, aggression rising like a storm front. His voice cut through the air, sharp, impatient, dangerous.

Then came the threat. He turned toward me, cigarette in hand, eyes narrowed, jaw tight. "I'll burn you with this," he said, the words low but edged, delivered in front of everyone—the couple, the driver, strangers nearby. The world seemed to pause, the heat pressing harder, the air thick with disbelief. My chest tightened, not from the sun but from the sudden awareness that safety had evaporated.

I stood still, calculating. The threat wasn't empty. I knew his volatility, the way anger could ignite without warning. My body braced, every nerve alert, the sun now secondary to the danger standing inches away. In that moment, survival became negotiation.

I decided quickly, silently. For personal safety, he would need marijuana. It didn't matter that it was illegal. The law was irrelevant when the choice was between escalation and containment. If drugs could dull the edge of his aggression, then compliance was the only path to calm.

The temple loomed ahead, ancient stone carved with stories of gods and battles, but all I could feel was the battle unfolding in the present. The ruins were timeless, but my reality was immediate: a cigarette held like a weapon, a threat delivered in daylight, and the knowledge that even here, surrounded by history and strangers, danger followed me.

Even family gatherings reinforced this control. His mother enabled him, shielding him from accountability, turning a blind eye to aggression, allowing him to change drinks throughout the night of his sister's wedding despite warnings. His siblings, friends, extended family—never confronting him, their avoidance a quiet form of acceptance. Silence became complicity.

The night of his sister's wedding he put the girls to bed, which was unheard of, as if he wanted to appear responsible. Later I found out he had done it without telling me. When I returned to the unit his mother had booked, I lay in bed with my daughters, watching TV on low volume, trying to calm myself. He came in, turned it off aggressively, and escalated. I contacted his mother, asking her to come and get me. I waited all night. She never came. Later she claimed she had, but I knew she hadn't.

The next morning my sister-in-law asked if I was okay. I told her no. She ignored me. His mother then dictated which cars we were to leave in, placing me in the same car with him and the children. He drove recklessly, each turn a dare against safety.

Driving became another vector of control. In a different state, with no support network, I had to ride with him and the children, watching him accelerate, feeling the threat in every movement. I sought help from his sister, staying back at her unit the following day while a wedding after-party barbecue was scheduled. I was happy for her to take the girls, but I explicitly stated she must care for them.

Ex returned to the unit during the barbecue. He tipped out my handbag in intimidation, then resorted to physical violence, kicking me in the back when I bent down to pick up my belongings. Dominance asserted; submission forced. The situation only calmed once he accessed marijuana.

It was relentless. Everyday life became a careful calculation of survival, every interaction a negotiation of threat and compliance. Financial dependence, substance misuse, aggression, and manipulation interlocked into a system designed to erode autonomy, fracture confidence, and claim control over every aspect of my existence.

Through it all, I carried shame. I concealed the chaos, curated appearances, and tried to compensate for the lack of order, morality, and empathy around me. Our children's social lives were limited—not for their sake, but because any exposure risked revealing cracks in the fragile façade we maintained. Outside, I appeared responsible, composed, moral. Inside, I was exhausted, second-guessing, constantly recalibrating.

I learned the patterns early, understood the scripts, and navigated them as best I could. Lies, omissions, coercion, threats, enabling by family and friends—they all formed a lattice of control, subtle and overt, leaving me questioning reality, questioning myself, and struggling to maintain even a semblance of normal life. My body carried it all—wired, aching, never released from vigilance, every muscle inscribed with survival.

Even when the house was quiet, even when the girls were asleep and the world seemed to hold its breath, I felt the weight of him pressing down. It wasn't always loud, or overt, or immediate. It was the subtle recalibration of my own instincts, the endless calculation of his moods, the shifting line between compliance and safety. Every word, every gesture, every look was measured—not because I wanted to, but because I had to.

I began to doubt everything I knew. My own memory, my own perception, my own truth. The most fundamental part of me—the one that prided itself on honesty—became a liability. When he accused me of lying, when he pointed to events and twisted them into evidence of my deceit, it struck at the very core of who I was. Truth, once a certainty, became a fragile artefact I could no longer rely on. And yet, I didn't lie. Not truly. I withheld, I navigated, I bent—not out of malice, but survival.

There were small moments, tiny fissures, where the gaslighting cut deepest. I recall returning from a visit with our daughter, Mia, who had asked for distance, who had set boundaries for herself. I carried her words carefully, tenderly—aware of the sharpness of truth in this household. And yet, after a dinner with his brother, where I elaborated on the exchange, the conversation twisted instantly. "You lied," he said. His tone, casual but corrosive, repeated over months.

Even as he hurled the accusation, I felt a quiet, almost imperceptible shift within me. My body no longer stiffened in the same instinctive fear. My spine carried a little more weight of certainty, my breath a little steadier, my eyes a touch firmer. The years of vigilance, of recalibrating every gesture, every word, every thought in anticipation of his manipulations, had not been wasted—they had forged a sense of presence that could no longer be fully hijacked.

I saw, more clearly than ever, the mechanics of his cruelty. The accusations, the subtle twists of truth, the insistence that reality itself had been reshaped—all were part of a façade he had spent decades perfecting. And yet, each time he spoke, each attempt to undermine me, the walls he had built to shield his lack of empathy trembled slightly. I could sense it, the imperfection in the performance.

It wasn't a triumphant moment. There was no cinematic release, no applause. It was quieter than that. It was a soft recognition, almost imperceptible in the space between my inhale and exhale. The grace I carried wasn't a shield I had crafted for others—it was mine, formed in the crucible of years spent navigating his volatility. My dignity wasn't dependent on his acknowledgement. My truth didn't require validation from a man who had long since forfeited the capacity to recognise it.

In that moment, I realised something profound: even within the claustrophobic architecture of manipulation, there was a locus of power that could not be taken, a core of self that remained untouched. It had been there all along, quietly observing, quietly enduring, quietly calibrating. The gaslighting, the coercion, the subtle assaults on my autonomy—they had tested me, stretched me, pushed me to the edges of doubt—but they had not annihilated me.

And as I recognised this, a strange clarity emerged. I began to see his actions not as reflections of my inadequacy, but as projections of his limitations. The cruelty, the manipulation, the constant undermining—they were tools of survival for him, not assessments of me. His lack of empathy, his relentless pursuit of control, became visible in sharp relief. And in that visibility, I found freedom—not immediate, not complete, but a freedom that rested in knowing the truth of myself.

My body, once taut with instinctive fear, began to settle in subtle ways. Shoulders dropped fractionally, chest eased, heart rate slowed. My nervous system, long in overdrive, began to remember what baseline felt like, even if only for fleeting moments. It was a quiet reclamation, almost imperceptible to the outside world, but monumental internally. For the first time in years, I felt the faint stirrings of calm not dictated by his behaviour, but by my own presence in my own body.

From that point, every encounter carried a different texture. I still moved carefully, still anticipated patterns, but the tension was tempered by awareness of the locus of control within me. Every accusation, every attempt to twist reality, became a test not of my truth, but of my endurance, of my capacity to hold presence, of my ability to exist with integrity under pressure.

It was subtle. It was internal. But it was revolutionary.

Even outside the home, the manipulation followed. Friends, acquaintances, family—they became instruments of isolation. My instinct to reach out, to share a concern, was tempered by the fear of disbelief, of ridicule, of dismissal. How could I speak when every assertion could be spun? Every memory could be questioned? Every truth could be weaponised against me?

Gaslighting wasn't always words. It was the calculated delay, the purposeful omission, the selective sharing of information. It was the way he would contradict me in front of others, turning social spaces into theatres of doubt. He did not need to scream, to shout, to strike. The uncertainty, the constant vigilance, the feeling that I could never be fully right—it was enough. It was enough to make me question reality. Enough to make me small, compliant, cautious.

And then there was the subtle violence—the threats that hovered at the edge of perception. Not always physical, but in every glance, in every smirk, in every tensioned breath. On trips, on dinners, on mundane errands, the pattern persisted. My body learned to read the flicker in his eyes before the words even formed. My heart beat faster at moments that should have been neutral. My stomach tightened, my hands trembled slightly when he lingered too long, when his presence loomed.

I began to recognise the choreography. He used proximity to unsettle me, silence to isolate me, allure to mislead everyone else. I learned, in those years, that the body doesn't forget. Even when I tried to convince myself that the environment was safe, even when logic whispered reassurance, my instincts bristled. I carried tension in the spaces between sentences, in the moments before the next step. My muscles remembered what my mind tried to forget.

Social appearances became an armour I could not remove. At gatherings, I maintained the mask of composure, the polished smile, the attentive listener. Inside, I was counting threats, recalculating potential danger, watching for micro-aggressions. He performed for the world—the good husband, the friend, the reliable son. Meanwhile, I juggled survival, negotiation, and protection. My daughters watched, learned, absorbed. The seeds of tension, of vigilance, were planted in their bodies too, even as I tried to shield them.

Sleep offered no respite. Nights were a time of subtle dread. Even in the dark, I imagined his movements, the potential for confrontation, the unspoken rules I must navigate. My dreams were fragmented, tense, filled with distorted echoes of reality. I awoke in the darkened house, listening, recalibrating, preparing for the day that had already begun in the quiet of my own body.

I had learned to live in the shadow of his unpredictability. I had learned to anticipate, to measure, to compromise endlessly. My autonomy shrank in increments, almost imperceptibly, until I realised I was navigating the world through his lens of perception. My identity, my confidence, my trust in my own judgment—they were all under siege, corroded by the slow drip of gaslighting, manipulation, and subtle, unrelenting aggression.

Even now, I can feel it—the taut line of vigilance threaded through my muscles, my posture, my breath. Even now, years later, I recognise the residue in the way I calculate words, the way I measure trust, the way I carry my children in the world. The psychological architecture of control leaves a footprint that time cannot erase, only layer over with memory, reflection, and reclaiming.

There are moments that don't look dramatic from the outside. No bruises. No shouting. No smashed walls or overturned chairs. Just a driveway, soft daylight, a pram leaning against brick. But sometimes those are the moments where control crystallises sharpest.

Before the girls were even one, there was a moment burned into me: Ex and my dad standing outside our house while I prepared to do the grocery shop. Two tiny bodies depending on me for absolutely everything. The weight of that re-sponsibility humming through my muscles like static electricity.

Ex and my dad were standing outside the house, talking. Nothing urgent, noth-ing important. Just idle conversation. I walked out, keys in my hand, the twin pram still unfolded behind me, and I asked Ex—gently, reasonably, completely exhausted—if he could look after **one** of the girls while I ran to the supermar-ket.

He didn't even look up properly.

Just that dismissive shrug, the flick of his voice,

"No. You're gonna have to do it at some point. May as well start now."

It wasn't loud.

It wasn't dramatic.

But it hit like a pressure clamp around my ribs—tightening, tightening.

Anyone who's wrangled even one baby knows how nerve-shredding a grocery run can be-let alone twins. The sounds, the juggling, the silent prayer that no meltdown begins in aisle three. Now double it. Add the logistics of twins. Mul-tiply by the weight of a partner who refuses to help—not out of inability, but out of entitlement.

The effort it took to get two babies out of the car, into the double pram, through narrow aisles, dodging stares, managing feeds and cries—it was a marathon every single time.

At mother's group I was always the first car in the car park and the last one to actually make it inside-twin logistics are their own full-body sport And when the meeting ended, I'd be first to say goodbye...

and the last to leave, wrestling with straps and buckles, the pram, the bags, the impossible weight of doing everything alone.

This was the invisible labour of my life.

This was the exhaustion no one applauded.

This was the cost of loving children inside a world built on someone else's power.

As they grew, the rhythms changed but the weight didn't.

Every morning, I dropped my girls at school.

Every afternoon, I drove the half hour to pick them up.

Those car rides became our decompression chamber, our truth-telling space, our tiny sanctuary from the storm.

They'd slide into the seats, breath still warm from the day.

We'd talk—about school, about friendships, about the small triumphs and fractures of growing up.

And sometimes, gently, about their dad.

They knew anger.

They knew emotional volatility.

But they didn't know about the marijuana, I shielded them from that part of him completely.

That was one secret I held tight, guarding their innocence like a fragile flame.

They knew he drank. They knew he smoked. But the drugs?

That truth didn't land until much later—long after eighteen.

I protected them from that world because I had to.

Because children should not have to carry their father's vices on their small, developing nervous systems.

So when I spoke about his aggression, his tone, the ways he pushed and manipulated and punished, they'd sit in the back seat and roll their eyes—not out of disrespect, but familiarity.

These conversations had become part of our survival script:

what's acceptable, what's not,

how to treat people,

how not to mistake volatility for love.

And despite everything they witnessed, everything they felt beneath the surface—the tension, the unpredictability, the heaviness in the air—they emerged with empathy. With boundaries. With clarity about how they deserve to be treated.

My girls will never mistake coercion for care.

They will never tolerate aggression as normal.

They will not stay silent for the sake of someone else's comfort.

And that... that is something I hold with pride in the deepest chambers of my chest.

Because even inside the most constricted, suffocating environment, something in me still fought to give them the blueprint I never had.

The map out of chaos.

The inner compass to choose differently.

The quiet knowledge that love should never require fear to function.

Chapter 4: Walking on Eggshells

⸻

Mornings arrived like a quiet drumbeat, each one carrying a frequency I had learned to read long before my eyes fully opened. Ex would rise, coffee in one hand, cigarette in the other, and I would feel the energy in the room like a barometer for the day ahead. Some days it hummed low and steady—safe enough to move through the house without flinching. Other days, the anger radiated off him in waves so sharp, I could feel it tighten my shoulders before I even spoke.

I learned to test the temperature with small gestures—a kiss on the cheek, a tentative question—and read the response like a map of danger. Distance became a reflex; I navigated around him as though each step might trigger a hidden fault line. Meanwhile, the girls relied on me for routines, breakfasts, travel, and care that stretched across long hours of traffic and errands. Every detail was a negotiation between the world outside and the microcosm of our home, where a misstep could ignite tension.

Even the dogs bore witness to this energy. One would tremble, urinate from anxiety, retreating from a presence that was meant to protect. I felt their silent betrayals acutely, every small act of fear mirroring my own. My attempts at gentle correction were swallowed by circumstance, the cumulative weight of fawning, testing, and compensating shaping each day into a high-stakes performance.

By evening, exhaustion settled in layers—muscles tight, mind alert, nerves fraying. I carried migraines and tension as markers of survival, my body translating stress into pain: sore fingers, elbows, shoulders, small warnings I learned not to ignore. Even the doctors could not see what my body already knew; only I could read the map of dysphoria, the subtle signals of trauma stored in every nerve, every joint. The quiet vigilance of daily life was a rhythm that left me simultaneously exhausted and hyper-aware, walking a path as fragile as a thread of glass stretched across the floor.

The mind can acclimate to danger long before the body ever agrees. The mind bargains, rationalises, explains things away. But the body—my body—kept score with a precision I couldn't escape. It whispered warnings long before my conscious brain was willing to admit anything was wrong. At times it didn't whisper at all; it screamed.

For years, I wore the exhaustion like a second skin, convinced it was just what life felt like. I told myself everyone felt like this—tight through the jaw, stiff in the shoulders, buzzing under the skin. I assumed most mothers lived on a steady drip of tension, always waiting for a shift in tone, a slammed cupboard, the wrong look. I thought it was just what it meant to be "strong."

But strength doesn't shake. Strength doesn't lie awake at 2 a.m. staring at a ceiling, waiting for footsteps. Strength doesn't flinch when keys turn in a lock. Strength doesn't fold its body into smaller and smaller shapes to become less visible, less noticeable, less confrontational.

No—this wasn't strength.

This was survival.

Hypervigilance woven into muscle and bone

The first sign was the constant scanning. I didn't know the word "hypervigilance" back then; I only felt the way my nervous system sat wired on high alert, like a radio tuned to static, searching for the faintest crackle of danger.

I'd wake up already mid-scan—listening to his footsteps, gauging the rhythm, the volume, the heaviness. I knew the mood before I even opened my eyes.

My body reacted faster than my thoughts. Shoulders tensing before my brain formed the words not safe. Breath shortening before I consciously noticed the shift in the room.

The body moves first-instinctive, ancient, unedited.

The intellect catches up later—sometimes years later.

I learned to "read" him with the accuracy of a seismograph detecting the first tremor of an earthquake. The twitch of a jaw. A muttered breath. The speed of a cigarette drag. The tone of a coffee cup placed just a little too hard on the counter. Micro-signals that meant nothing to others... but meant everything to me.

My stomach would tighten, a deep subterranean clench—like my organs bracing themselves. The muscles in my back would seize, pulling my shoulders towards my ears until I eventually adopted it as my natural posture: head down, shoulders lifted, neck shortened. A human shield trying to fold itself inward.

Later, when I found Pat Ogden's (2015) work on somatic therapy, I recognised myself instantly in the descriptions: the "turtling," the shrinking, the protective stance of someone who is both frozen and waiting to flee. But at the time, it didn't feel psychological. It felt physical. Purely physical. As if my skeleton had re-shaped itself into vigilance.

You don't have to be hit to become afraid; unpredictability is its own form of impact.

You don't have to be chased to run.

You just have to live inside unpredictability long enough.

The fear of being "dramatic"

The worst part wasn't the tension—it was the shame that shadowed it.

The way I'd second guess every instinct.

Am I overreacting?

Am I imagining this?

Is it really that bad?

Maybe it's me.

Maybe I'm the problem.

Conditioning works slowly and quietly. I had been trained, over years, to distrust my own perception. To downplay what happened. To swallow it. To normalise it.

So the first time I saw the police, I was prepared them to take a statement, but not respond with as much weight to my predicament. When I gave my statement—hands cold, voice shaking—they looked at me with a seriousness I wasn't prepared for.

"This is dangerous," one of them said. "You're not imagining it."

Their words landed with a force I had never allowed myself to feel inside my own home. Because it validated what my body had been screaming for years.

The second time I went—after he threatened to put me through a wall and kick my dog—I felt the same war inside myself. The minimising. The self-doubt. The shame. And again, the police didn't wave it off. They were concerned.

And in that moment, I realised something horrifying:

I had become numb to danger.

So numb that I needed strangers in uniform to tell me when I was unsafe.

Years of conditioning can do that. It's like the body absorbs the shock so the mind can continue to function. But eventually, the container cracks.

When the body breaks the silence

My body had its own language. At first, it was subtle—headaches, random pains, fatigue I couldn't shake. Then came the migraines. The stabbing gut pain. The sudden inability to sleep. The trembling in my hands. The sensation of running on adrenaline while also feeling entirely numb.

Then came something even stranger. Something I didn't have a name for.

Stress would collect in one tiny place—like the tip of my pointer finger. Just the one finger. It would ache, then throb, then burn. And if I ignored it, the pain would migrate—wrist, elbow, shoulder—spreading through the arm as if my body was escalating the alert.

Pay attention.

Slow down.

Listen.

But I didn't. I kept going. I kept minimising. And eventually, I found myself in Emergency, shoulder locked in pain so intense I couldn't sleep.

At work, they assumed I was exaggerating. I saw the looks. The silent judgment. The disbelief. Even when the doctor sent me for x-rays, nothing showed up. No RSI. No fractures. No inflammation.

A few years later I read Robert Scaer's The Trauma Spectrum.

Cumulative trauma dysphoria.

The body holding stress in ways that look invisible on scans but feel catastrophic inside.

I didn't need a diagnosis.

I needed someone to tell me my body wasn't lying.

IBS: the alarm system I never asked for

The worst physical symptom—the one that would paralyse me completely—was the IBS. That deep, twisting gut pain that felt less like digestion and more like a siren.

One day stands out above all the others. We were going to couples counselling—a session we left halfway through to return to our concrete manufacturing factory and finish a pour. He said he was fine. Calm. Safe.

My body violently disagreed.

Pain hit like lightning. I dropped into a crouch, gripping a heavy board.

Instinctive. Primal. A posture I had never taken before in my life.

Low. Small. Compact. Protected.

I thought of a bilby—those tiny Australian marsupials that freeze when threatened. That was me: frozen, hunched, clutching that board like it was a shield.Each time I tried to stand, the pain returned, a burning twist that shoved me right back down.

Stay small.

Stay low.

Don't stand tall.

Don't be visible.

Don't provoke.

My body knew something before I did.

And it wasn't subtle.

The posture of a hunted person

It wasn't until much later, reading and learning about trauma, that I realised I had built a lifelong posture around fear. Even as a teenager—head down, fringe covering my face, oversized jumper hanging off my shoulders—I'd been trying to shrink myself. Trying not to attract attention. Trying not to be a target.

I didn't stand upright; I folded inward.

I didn't take up space; I disappeared into it.

Even now, I struggle to know what "standing straight" feels like. My head naturally tilts back too far, overcompensating for years of hunching. A friend once pointed out that it was a balance issue—the body trying to correct patterns it learned decades ago.

And she was right: the body remembers what the mind forgets.

You can see it in people on the street if you look closely. The forward slump of someone who carries years of stress. The tightened jaw of someone who anticipates conflict. The brow crease of someone who has spent too much time confused or frightened. Even that hump at the base of the neck—often called a "buffalo hump"—linked to chronic high cortisol levels.

Trauma etches itself into posture, into gait, into breath.

The body becomes the biography.

Sleep: the battleground

Sleep wasn't rest.

It was a negotiation.

Some nights, I'd lie rigid, listening for shifts in breathing beside me. Listening for movement. Listening for the tone of the house—yes, even homes have tones.

Some nights, I didn't dream at all. My system stayed too activated to fully drop down. It's a known trauma response: the nervous system refuses to enter deep sleep because deep sleep equals vulnerability.

The breaking point

There wasn't one dramatic meltdown. No collapse. No screaming or crying on a bathroom floor. My breaking point was quieter than that.

It was a Tuesday night. Nothing extraordinary. I was in bed, Ex and I had only the day before been separated by an IVO. A pressure entered my body, in the chest and the upper gut area, at times entering my throat. I had thought indigestion, following two paracetamol and ibuprofen not long before, so I got up to have an ice-cream to attempt to settle the pain. A long and restless night continued. The pain remaining into the morning, I had breakfast, once again hoping that it would dissipate the symptoms. Nothing happened. Due to recent high blood pressure, I thought it could be my heart.

My gut bloated.

My chest tightened.

My breath stuttered.

I wasn't crying. I wasn't panicking in the dramatic sense.

I was... collapsing.

But not physically.

Neurologically.

Emotionally.

Systemically.

My body had finally had enough.

Years of swallowed fear.

Years of minimising danger.

Years of shrinking, turtling, crouching.

Years of waiting for safety that never came.

This wasn't weakness.

This wasn't fragility.

This was the body refusing to absorb one more ounce of threat.

I sat down. Slowly. Carefully.

And for the first time in my adult life, I didn't push through.

I didn't override it.

I didn't try to be "fine."

I listened.

And in that listening, something inside me unclenched—not relief, not freedom, but recognition.

The body was saying:

Enough.

You're hurting me.

You're hurting us.

And we can't keep living like this.

That morning, lying on the couch, I felt every muscle trembling under my skin. A soft vibration, like the aftershock of an earthquake. My jaw pulsed. My stomach ached. My shoulders curled up toward my ears without permission.

My breath was shallow.

My chest tight.

My thoughts foggy.

And for the first time—not from fear of him but from fear of my own internal collapse—I whispered into the dark:

"I think my body is breaking."

Not my mind.

Not my spirit.

My body.

It had carried me through too much for too long-and it was finally buckling.

I had realised long ago trauma doesn't just live in memories.

It lives in muscles.

In fascia.

In breath.

In posture.

In the organs.

In the gut.

In the skin.

In the way you stand.

In the way you flinch.

In the way you brace for impact even when no one is raising a hand.

But I though this may be my breaking point.

It was the culmination of a thousand tiny violences—some loud, some silent—all absorbed by a body that had been trying to protect me from the truth.

The truth that danger doesn't have to be constant to be effective.

It only has to be unpredictable.

And my body had known that long before I did.

It wasn't the heart—only the gut screaming back. Seven hours of tests, ECGs, needles, antacids, a quiet discharge.

The diagnosis didn't capture the truth. My body had spoken louder than any chart, and for the first time, I acknowledged it.

The mind becomes its own interrogator. Every thought questioned, every impulse scrutinised. I started noticing it in the small decisions first. Should I respond to that text, or leave it? Did I say something the wrong way, or was he projecting again? A casual comment in the hallway could spiral into hours of mental debate. My mind, once confident, now sifted through every memory, every interaction, searching for proof that I was at fault.

Am I overreacting?

Did I cause this?

Was my tone wrong? My expression too sharp?

It became a constant negotiation, a balancing act between self-preservation and morality. The logic of right and wrong blurred. I could feel myself bending inward, trying to anticipate the world before it even arrived, to pre-empt the storm I was convinced I had conjured. Guilt became an echo in every thought. I would replay conversations, gestures, decisions, and imagine dozens of ways I had failed—even when objectively nothing had happened.

Trust in my own perception eroded. I doubted not only him but myself. If my own judgment couldn't be trusted, who could I turn to? Each time I convinced myself I was imagining it, that I was being dramatic, that self-doubt etched another layer into my psyche. And yet, beneath that doubt, something else lingered—an instinct I no longer recognised, whispering that my internal alarms were not lies.

The quietest moments were the hardest. Walking alone down the street, I would feel a flicker of anxiety without reason, the shadow of his presence lingering in my chest. Every sound, a potential signal. Every look, an assessment. My mind became a courtroom, my memories witnesses, and I was both accused and judge.

I learned to negotiate with myself. Calm the racing thoughts. Convince the instinct to silence itself. Rationalise the anxiety away. And yet, like water against stone, doubt seeped through every barrier.

And then, small acts of resistance began. Tiny, almost imperceptible moments where

I didn't second-guess completely.

I paused before apologising for things I hadn't done.

I noted a thought without surrendering it.

I acknowledged my own feelings without labelling them as wrong.

These moments were brief, fragile sparks—but they hinted at something I hadn't felt in years: trust in myself, even if only in fragments.

It was here, in the unremarkable edges of daily life, that I first realised resistance was possible. Not the dramatic confrontations of movies, not a sudden eruption of defiance—but a quiet, internal claiming of space. My thoughts began to whisper that perhaps the mind could be trained to listen to itself again. That perhaps the erosion of self-trust wasn't permanent.

And in that whisper, the faintest pulse of strength returned, setting the stage for something larger, something I would recognise later as the beginning of re-claiming myself.

Have you ever felt the weight of walking on eggshells? Not the literal kind, not the clattering of ceramic underfoot, but the invisible kind that presses against your chest, squeezes your stomach, tugs at your shoulders, and never lets go. The kind that teaches you to move carefully, to choose words like stepping stones over a fragile bridge, to pause, assess, and calculate before even thinking about acting.

That was my life. Not in a single explosive moment, but in thousands of small ones that accumulated, layer upon layer. The quiet sighs, the slight shift of tone, the tightening of the jaw I learned to see from across a room. Every gesture was a clue, every glance a signal. And I, trained by circumstance, learned to interpret them with precision—but at what cost?

Externally, life looked ordinary. A tidy home, the routine of work, the small rituals that suggested calm and normalcy. But inside, the body held the story the mind tried to smooth over. A hand hovering a millimetre above a cup to test the reaction. A breath caught mid-inhale. Shoulders lifted just slightly, to be smaller, to disappear. The world saw composure; my body told another story entirely.

And yet, amid the tension, I found the tiniest acts of survival. A smile offered at the wrong moment that kept things calm. A joke told softly, diverting attention. Leaving the room for just a few minutes, claiming it as mundane necessity while it was really a strategic retreat. These were not heroics; they were methods of self-preservation. They were quiet ways to carve out space, to claim just enough oxygen to keep moving forward.

I wonder, how many of us live in this way without even realising it? We carry the invisible weight of fear or anticipation, the delicate balance between loyalty, love, and self-protection. It may not be a toxic partner; it could be a demanding parent, a manipulative friend, a workplace that thrives on fear, or even our own internalised pressure. The physical, emotional, and mental strains are the same. The body responds before the mind registers, the instincts keep tally, and the small acts of negotiation—the pauses, the shifts, the micro-decisions—become survival tactics.

Even so, the tension does not crush entirely. It teaches subtle resilience. It sharpens observation. It awakens awareness. The very act of noticing, of pausing, of recognising what is happening inside oneself, becomes the foundation for reclaiming agency. And that is where hope begins, not in grand gestures, but in noticing the small spaces where choice still exists.

I ask you now, reader: have you ever paused to notice your own survival moves? The ways you bend or hold back to protect yourself? The ways you perform composure while your body hums a different story? What does it feel like when your internal world is at odds with the external, and how often do you allow yourself to recognise that dissonance?

There is intimacy in that recognition. A subtle solidarity that connects one human being to another across time and circumstance. Even when we feel alone, these threads of internal experience—fear, caution, doubt, anticipation—are universal. They echo in countless lives, shaped differently but understood instinctively.

And here is the quiet suspense: even in the constant tension, even in the moments where the body speaks and the mind questions, there is growth. Awareness of the pattern is the first whisper of resistance. The smallest acknowledgement—pausing instead of reacting, noting instead of swallowing—becomes a foothold. A tiny act of agency that hints at something more. Something beyond survival.

The tension remains. The eggshells still crack underfoot.

But the noticing changes everything.

It shifts the narrative from unconscious endurance to conscious navigation.

From complete submission to careful negotiation. From erosion to the faintest spark of reclamation.

And it is that spark, barely visible but undeniable, that will lead me forward. Not yet a blaze, but enough to illuminate the path toward something greater: the reclamation of self, the recognition of boundaries, the slow and deliberate return to a body and mind that listen to each other, that honour instinct, that trust perception.

Until then, we walk. Carefully, consciously, but with awareness. And awareness is the first step toward resilience.

There were nights when the house felt like it was holding its breath—walls tight, floorboards tense, air heavy with something unsaid but unmistakable. That's what living with him was like. Not chaos, not storms, but pressure. A slow encroaching hush before a strike. A suspense that lived in the body long before the mind could name it. And the most chilling part was always this: **he knew exactly what he was doing.**

He carried his power like a shadow stretching over every room. He didn't need to shout.. Sometimes a look was enough. A narrowed gaze. A flicker of disgust crossing his face. A shift in posture that signalled danger the way animals sense a predator under the brush. Every gesture echoed with deliberate meaning. He knew how to stand just a bit too close, how to tilt his head so the threat landed like a blade in slow motion. He knew how fear worked in the nervous system—how it seeped into the muscles, the chest, the breath. And he used that knowledge the way other men use tools.

There were moments he liked to escalate, tiny tests disguised as accidents. A slammed door that rattled the frame. The reckless turn of the steering wheel with the car accelerating just enough to make my stomach drop. He understood physics, adrenaline, the edge between safety and harm. He knew how to make me afraid without ever leaving a mark.

But intimidation was only one layer. He preferred something more elegant: control. Quiet, consuming control that seeped into finances, decisions, movements, relationships. It was never random. It was crafted.

He'd take my bank cards "accidentally."

Money wasn't his concern — it was mine. I rationed every dollar, tucking notes into hiding spots around the house to cover bills. He'd steal it anyway, vanish for hours, and return with stories that never matched the truth: it was always for drugs.

He knew the power of taking what I'd painstakingly hidden.

He knew the strategy in making me scramble, hunt, and worry over money meant for the family.

He knew what it did to a nervous system already trained to survive, to anticipate, to comply.

He manipulated money the way he manipulated emotions—precise, calculated, and ruthless. He'd lose money, hide money, make decisions without me, then turn around and blame me for the fallout. When bills weren't paid, it was my fault. When debts appeared out of nowhere, it was because I'd "failed to supervise." He knew the psychological impact of scarcity—how it tightens the mind, shrinks the future, and traps the body in survival mode.

He used the same method with affection.

Give nothing.

Take everything.

Then demand gratitude.

His emotional cruelty wasn't impulsive. It was strategic.

He knew exactly when to deploy humiliation—when eyes were watching.

He knew the timing of the silent treatment—long enough to destabilise, short enough to deny.

He knew how to twist a sentence until I questioned my own memory.

He knew how to cut me off mid-speech, then accuse me of being the one who didn't listen.

He weaponised inconsistency like an art form.

Love dangled like a key just out of reach.

Approval rationed like oxygen.

Identity dismantled piece by piece.

He even tampered with spirituality—not directly at first, but through smirks, ridicule, disdain that landed sharper than any insult. He knew faith was personal, so he attacked it quietly, sideways, with comments designed to erode rather than confront.

The children weren't spared from his strategy.

Never overtly—never in a way that could be photographed or recorded—but in ways that altered the temperature of the house.

He used them as messengers when he wanted distance.

He used them as shields when he wanted access.

He used them as leverage when he wanted control.

They learned early how to read his moods, how to step around his expectations, how to predict the tone of the night from the tension in his jaw. He knew they were watching. He knew children absorb what they see long before what they're told. And still, he used them anyway.

One evening, just after dinner, I asked him to take his plate to the sink. My daughter froze mid-bite, her eyes wide and trembling with a fear I had long since felt in my own body. She looked at me as if I'd asked the impossible, her thoughts unspoken but sharp as knives: *Mum, why would you do that? You're going to make him angry.* The air seemed to tighten around us, charged with the knowledge that a simple request could trigger a storm. Even at her young age, she had learned the quiet calculus of survival, reading his moods with the precision of a seasoned observer, anticipating the danger before it even arrived.

Sometimes he used danger as a language—pursuing cars on the road with rage thick enough to choke on, threatening other drivers while the children sat frozen and silent in the backseat. He knew the fear it created. He relied on it.

And when violence crossed the threshold—when pushing turned into grabbing, when shoving turned into pinning, when poking turned into kicking—he knew the escalation wasn't an accident. It never is. Men like him don't "snap." They calculate. They climb a ladder they built step by step.

But his favourite tactic—the one he polished until it gleamed—was blame.

He'd twist reality until it buckled.

He'd deny what he'd done even minutes after doing it.

He'd minimise every act, every threat, every bruise on the inside of my body.

He'd point to my reactions as the "real problem."

He knew exactly how to scramble my sense of cause and effect.

He used jealousy as a justification.

He used envy as a disguise for control.

He used "love" as a shield that hid his intent.

And after the abuse, after the rage, after the chaos, he'd stand there with empty hands and a clean face, insisting he wasn't responsible. Insisting I made him do it. Insisting I provoked him. Insisting the whole thing was a misunderstanding. He knew the script and he played it flawlessly.

And still—he'd threaten to leave.

Threaten to end his own life.

Threaten to sell the house from under me.

Threaten to ruin everything if I stepped out of line.

He knew threats activate the deepest survival circuits.

He knew what fear does to a person raised on compliance.

He knew exactly how to pull the strings.

He treated me like property because he believed he owned me—my time, my decisions, my body.

And when he refused to parent, refused to help, refused to care, he knew that too was a tactic. Neglect disguised as incompetence. Helplessness wielded as power.

At the same time, he created a version of himself he presented to the world—reasonable, hardworking, misunderstood. He used this façade like armour. He counted on others believing it. He crafted this narrative so perfectly that he believed he could act without consequence.

But deep down, beneath the surface, one truth held steady:

He knew. He always knew.

Every choice was calculated.

Every escalation was intentional.

Every silence was a strategy.

Every threat was a tool.

Every act of cruelty was deliberate.

He built a system of control, and he expected everyone—me, the children, the world—to orbit around it. When he looked at us, he didn't see humans with needs or dreams or fear. He saw instruments. Extensions of himself. Objects to be directed, managed, manipulated.

But here is the part he didn't predict:

My body was keeping the score.

My intuition was taking notes.

My nervous system was memorising every shift in the air.

My daughters were watching, learning, calculating their own escape routes.

The legacy he thought he was writing was already fracturing.

Because there comes a moment in every psychological thriller where the protagonist stops whispering and starts seeing clearly. When the patterns no longer confuse. When the fog lifts just enough to show the shape of the monster.

He believed he could bend reality forever.

He was wrong.

When the financial abuse reached its peak, it wasn't just numbers on a statement—it was a stand-over, a constant pressure that crept into every corner of the house. Threats hovered behind every request for money, the underlying message clear: give it up, or face his rage. The money he extracted wasn't for bills or necessities—it was for drugs, for the impulses that never cared about the chaos left in their wake. Eventually, the inevitable happened: his violence landed him in jail.

For a brief flicker of hope, I believed things had changed when we tried to put the pieces back together. I opened a separate account, a small island of control in a storm of manipulation. But even then, the financial responsibility fell squarely on me. I carried the weight of the bills: rates, electricity, water, the mortgage. His private health insurance became another impossible demand; I cancelled it for him, unable to keep it afloat, but I held on for myself—and for the girls—protecting them from the collateral damage of his recklessness. I paid for their coverage until they reached the age limit, my own measure of safety in a household where control had long been a weapon.

Chapter 5: The Making of a Storm

———

After years of carrying the financial load, something in me kept asking the same question: How did he become this way? That question became the bridge into understanding the world that shaped him long before he ever stepped into mine.

Researchers like Allan Schore (2019) highlight that boys are biologically more vulnerable to early stress. Increased prenatal testosterone combined with maternal stress elevates cortisol exposure in the womb, altering how stress circuits wire and leaving lasting imprints on emotional regulation and impulse control. Boys exposed to these conditions are more likely to display aggression, defiance, and heightened anger, particularly in environments lacking attuned caregiving. Studies show that boys raised in single-mother households exhibit nearly twice the rate of behavioural problems compared with boys in two-parent families—evidence that biology and environment collide to shape early behaviour long before a child can understand it.

From the very start, Ex's life unfolded on precarious ground, teetering between chaos and survival. His mother, stressed while pregnant, exposed him to neurological risks that would later manifest as ADHD, impulsivity, and difficulty with focus. Concentration was never his ally. In classrooms, the struggle was constant—teachers' notes a litany of challenges: "Ex has made reasonable progress but still lacks the ability to concentrate for long periods," "frequently lacks concentration," "needs extra motivation to complete tasks," "easily distracted." Even bursts of focus or sporting success were fleeting; discipline was inconsistent, and the margins for error narrow.

Home offered no refuge. Ex's mother, emotionally scarred from her own childhood, was still a child herself in many ways—ill-equipped to provide guidance, structure, or safety. The household was dominated by a violent, alcoholic stepfather. Ex, the eldest, assumed responsibility far beyond his years. By age three, he had climbed onto his stepfather's back to shield his mother during acts of extreme violence. By six, he ran away from home—alone—multiple times, only to be returned by the police. After his parents' separation, he became a caretaker to his siblings: cooking, cleaning, and keeping them safe. A child acting as parent, navigating his own trauma while trying to survive the chaos around him.

Before he even understood the world, Ex and his siblings were thrust into dangers no child should bear. In the 1980s, gang violence flared in their neighbourhood. His stepdad would send his mother with the kids into the middle of it, ordering her to rescue his sister from a possible gunfight. Ex watched the panic in her eyes, felt adrenaline spike in his small body, and learned that danger wasn't abstract—it could erupt at any moment. Childhood became a minefield of unpredictability, where adult decisions—and adult recklessness—could place them directly in harm's way. Survival meant bending every rule, ignoring fear, thinking fast before life—or death—caught up with you.

Much of the time, Ex was left alone. His mother worked night shifts, exhausted, chasing just five more minutes of sleep. The house, dimly lit and silent, became a testing ground for responsibility far beyond his years. He fed his siblings, ensured they got to school, and tried to keep the house functional. Supervision was scarce, and boundaries blurred; the line between survival and misbehaviour was almost invisible.

Poverty pressed on Ex from every angle. The poorest suburbs surrounded him—streets littered with crime, broken glass glinting under streetlights, sirens wailing in the distance. Essentials were scarce; sometimes there wasn't enough to eat, and shoes or clothing were patched, handed down, improvised. He learned early that the world would not cushion him, and survival often meant bending rules just to get by.

School offered no sanctuary either. Ex endured punitive teachers, humiliation, and physical aggression. One teacher tore his earring out, leaving him shaken and confused. Early reports reflected the tension between potential and struggle: "Ex has settled down well into grade two work... but his standard is below grade level." By grade four, the reports were unmistakable: "Frequently lacks concentration," "needs extra motivation to complete tasks," "easily distracted." Impulsivity, poor attention regulation, and weak inhibition remained, sometimes masked by sporting success or fleeting engagement. Consequences were abstract. When trouble arose, his mother often negotiated with schools, shielding him from full accountability. Immediate survival, stimulation, or action took precedence over foresight or restraint.

Risk and rebellion became almost inevitable. One incident stands out as a mark on his adolescent record: the stolen car. Barely old enough to reach the pedals, Ex climbed into the neighbour's car for an illicit joyride, his younger brother working the pedals. They managed to circle the block and sneak the car back into the driveway, hearts pounding, only to be caught the instant they pulled up. Escaping serious injury, but the act became emblematic of a deeper pattern. He had already internalised lessons about bending rules, taking risks, and disregarding consequences. The streets, the poverty, and the constant need to fend for himself had created a young boy for whom legality was fluid and survival paramount.

Trauma compounded every aspect of Ex's development. Molested by his uncle and later discredited by his mother, he internalised a dangerous lesson: speak up, and you will be dismissed or shamed. Physical abuse was constant. Electrical cords left scars on his core, while emotional neglect and lack of guidance became normalised. He wandered streets unsupervised, nearly injured himself breaking into an empty house, and was introduced to marijuana by his stepfather—a foundation for risk-taking and substance use that would shadow him into adulthood.

And yet, glimpses of potential shimmered. Moments of intelligence, athletic success, and fleeting focus suggested a child who, given structure, safety, and attunement, could thrive. But the imprint of trauma—the parental neglect, domestic violence, and lack of accountability—left permanent marks. Patterns learned in childhood—impulsivity, poor inhibition, emotional dysregulation—echoed throughout adulthood, shaping relationships, work, and parenting.

Ex's impulsivity, impatience, and disregard for consequences became engrained. He could not sit still, could not wait his turn, and laughed off statements made without filter or forethought. Driving became an arena of risk—speeding, ignoring rules, putting himself and others in danger. Poor time management required alarms and external prompts, yet crisis was inevitable when systems failed. Financial foresight was foreign; he would spend an entire week's wages on the day it arrived, leaving necessities, bills, and family responsibilities in jeopardy. Impulse buying, substance use, and lack of planning were survival mechanisms rooted in a childhood where chaos reigned.

zWork was a battleground. Jobs were lost not from lack of skill, but from impulsivity, intolerance of authority, and difficulty sustaining focus. Truck driving became untenable after repeated speeding fines threatened his license. Self-employment offered temporary relief, providing immediate consequences he could navigate and control, yet long-term structure remained elusive. Relationships mirrored these patterns. Communication was poor, support inconsistent, and mood swings unpredictable. He struggled to be present for his children, overwhelmed by even simple domestic or financial responsibilities.

Ex's emotional blueprint was a patchwork of trauma and survival. Anxiety and depression shadowed him, long periods spent in bed despite partial help from medication. Impulsivity fused with thrill-seeking and substance use. Blind to long-term consequences, his shallow emotional reach left neglect in its wake—for himself and anyone within orbit. He acted without reflection, prioritising immediate need, stimulation, or survival, as he had learned from a young age.

These experiences were not isolated. They threaded through his upbringing, shaping reckless impulses, thrill-seeking behaviours, and disregard for authority that would follow him into adulthood. Poverty, neglect, and exposure to crime were crucibles forging patterns that would later manifest as impulsivity, deceit, and a willingness to flout rules when it served immediate needs.

This story is not a justification, nor does it absolve Ex of responsibility. But it illuminates the mechanics of generational and environmental impact, showing how trauma, neglect, and exposure to violence carve deep channels in the psyche. Understanding these roots provides context: why he acts impulsively, struggles with control, and navigates relationships with difficulty. It reveals the collision of biology, environment, and learned behaviour, showing how trauma and neurodevelopment shape not just a child, but an adult, and how these patterns ripple across the lives he touches.

For those reading, this chapter offers more than a recounting of events; it provides a lens into the subtle inheritance of chaos, the consequences of early trauma, and the patterns that, left unchecked, can manifest across a lifetime. Recognising these patterns is the first step toward intervention, insight, and, ultimately, breaking cycles before they extend into the next generation.

PCL-R Traits Checklist The PCL-R (Psychopathy Checklist–Revised) is a psychological assessment tool used by trained forensic psychologists, psychiatrists, and other qualified professionals to evaluate the presence of psychopathic & sociopathic traits and behaviours in individuals, often in criminal justice or clinical settings. Note: This is not a diagnosis. The experiences below are personal observations and examples.

Glibness/Superficial Charm: *Does the individual use charm, flattery, or smooth talk to gain trust or manipulate others?*

Ex did not possess true charm or polish. What he did have was a kind of surface-level talkativeness, often inserting himself into conversations without real understanding, repeating things he'd heard from others, or pushing opinions he barely knew anything about. He sometimes seemed to attempt influence, but it was clumsy and unrefined rather than smooth or alluring.

Grandiose Sense of Self-Worth: *Does the individual have an inflated sense of self-importance and believe they are superior to others?*

Ex regularly displayed an inflated sense of self-importance, particularly within family interactions. He misread social cues, often assuming admiration or attraction where none existed, reflecting a disconnect between his perception of himself and how others experienced him.

Need for Stimulation/Proneness to Boredom: *Does the individual crave excitement and easily get bored with routine activities?*

Ex became quickly bored and disliked routine. His thrill-seeking behaviours, from reckless driving to risky childhood antics such as shoplifting batteries, demonstrate a craving for stimulation that sometimes led to illegal behaviours.

Pathological Lying: *Does the individual lie frequently and convincingly, often without remorse?*

Ex was a habitual liar. He lied even about trivial matters, repeatedly breaking trust. Lying functioned as a survival mechanism, ingrained from patterns learned early in life, rather than as calculated manipulation.

Conning/Manipulativeness: *Does the individual exploit others for personal gain through deception or manipulation?*

Ex exploited others for personal gain, especially in situations where he required assistance. He frequently used circumstances to manipulate resources or support to suit his immediate needs.

Lack of Remorse or Guilt: *Does the individual lack remorse for their actions and show no guilt, even when harming others?*

Ex showed minimal genuine remorse. Requests to recognise or amend harmful behaviour were often ignored. He repeated behaviours that caused harm without meaningful reflection or accountability.

Shallow Affect: *Does the individual show a limited range of emotions or a lack of emotional depth?*

Ex's emotional range was very limited. He struggled to connect with others in a meaningful way and rarely displayed depth of feeling. Genuine warmth, vulnerability, or empathy were largely absent, and he seemed unable to experience or express the kind of emotional reciprocity that forms authentic bonds.

Callous Lack of Empathy: *Does the individual lack empathy or concern for the feelings of others?*

Ex displayed minimal empathy. He frequently dismissed or mocked the feelings of others, including disclosures of trauma or abuse, revealing a consistent inability to relate to or comfort others.

Poor Behavioural Controls: *Does the individual lack impulse control and often engage in reckless or irresponsible behaviour?*

Ex had poor behavioural control. Anger, impulsivity, and risky behaviours—such as dangerous driving and thrill-seeking on motorcycles—demonstrated difficulty managing impulses and assessing consequences.

Need for Thrill/Lack of Responsibility: *Does the individual crave excitement and risk-taking and show little regard for the consequences?*

Ex sought excitement and frequently neglected responsibility. Household duties and family obligations were often ignored in favour of immediate stimulation or personal gratification.

Parasitic Lifestyle: *Does the individual exploit others for their resources and avoid taking responsibility for their actions?*

Ex exhibited a parasitic lifestyle, relying on others to cover essential expenses while contributing selectively only when convenient or beneficial to him.

Early Behavioural Problems: *Did the individual exhibit conduct problems or aggression early in life?*

Ex displayed early conduct problems, including aggression toward siblings, breaking into vacant houses, and early exposure to illegal substances introduced by his stepfather.

Lack of Realistic Long-Term Goals: *Does the individual lack clear goals or aspirations for the future?*

Ex showed minimal long-term planning. He reacted to immediate problems rather than proactively managing responsibilities, rarely considering the broader consequences of his actions.

Impulsivity: *Does the individual act impulsively without considering the consequences?*

Ex acted impulsively throughout life. Threats of violence, reckless decisions, and rash behaviour illustrate a pattern of immediate action without reflection on outcomes.

Irresponsibility: *Does the individual fail to meet their obligations or commitments?*

Ex frequently failed to fulfil obligations or commitments, whether legal agreements, financial responsibilities, or household duties, leaving others to manage the consequences.

Juvenile Delinquency: *Has the individual engaged in criminal behaviour during their youth?*

Ex engaged in early criminal behaviours, including stealing a neighbour's car for a joyride, breaking into a vacant house, and experimenting with marijuana introduced by his stepfather.

Adult Antisocial Behaviour: *Has the individual engaged in criminal or illegal activities as an adult?*

Ex engaged in adult criminal or illegal behaviours, including substance abuse, family violence, theft, and reckless driving, demonstrating a sustained disregard for rules and safety.

Promiscuous Sexual Behaviour: *Does the individual have a history of casual and short-term sexual relationships?*

Ex did not engage in casual sexual relationships during the period observed. While he occasionally sought attention or flirtation from others, there is no evidence of sexual activity outside the relationship. His behaviour reflected a desire for validation and excitement rather than promiscuity.

Many Short-Term Marital Relationships: *Has the individual had multiple short-term marriages or relationships?*

Ex has had only one marriage, beginning at age 20, with a long-term relationship marked by sociopathic behaviours that profoundly impacted the partnership.

Interpretation:

- Scores of 0-10 indicate minimal or no psychopathic traits.

- Scores of 11-20 suggest some psychopathic traits, but not to a clinically significant degree.

- Scores of 21-30 indicate moderate to high levels of psychopathic traits, potentially impacting relationships and life functioning.

• Scores of 31-40 suggest high levels of psychopathy, with significant risk of antisocial behaviour and lack of empathy.

To provide a measure of impartiality, I ran my observations through ChatGPT to simulate a structured scoring of the PCL-R checklist. Based on the answers I provided, it generated an overall rating of **31–33/40**, indicating high levels of psychopathic traits and a significant risk of antisocial behaviour and lack of empathy. This exercise was not a clinical diagnosis, but a way to objectively assess the patterns I observed.

Using the 3-point scale (0 = Does not apply, 1 = Applies somewhat, 2 = Definitely applies), Ex's behaviours align with the following traits:

• **Allure/Surface-Level Influence:** 1–2 – Ex lacked true depth or polish in interactions. He occasionally repeated what others said, giving the impression of knowledge he didn't truly have.

• **Grandiose Sense of Self-Worth:** 2 – He often overestimated his importance, misreading social cues and believing others were more attracted or impressed by him than they were.

• **Need for Stimulation/Proneness to Boredom:** 2 – Easily bored, seeking excitement through thrill-seeking, reckless driving, and childhood shoplifting.

• **Pathological Lying:** 2 – Lies were frequent, often unnecessary, and served as a survival or manipulation tool rather than considered deception.

• **Conning/Manipulativeness:** 2 – He regularly exploited others for resources or convenience, using circumstances to manipulate outcomes.

• **Lack of Remorse or Guilt:** 2 – Little evidence of genuine remorse; harmful behaviours were repeated without reflection.

• **Shallow Affect:** 2 – Limited emotional depth, struggling to connect meaningfully with others or recognise emotional reciprocity.

• **Callous Lack of Empathy:** 2 – Demonstrated minimal concern for others' feelings, often mocking or dismissing distress, even during disclosures of trauma.

• **Poor Behavioural Controls:** 2 – Impulsivity, anger, and risky behaviours, such as dangerous motorcycle rides and reckless driving, were consistent.

• **Need for Thrill/Lack of Responsibility:** 2 – Craved excitement and often neglected obligations, leaving shared tasks unfinished.

• **Parasitic Lifestyle:** 2 – Avoided financial and practical responsibilities, relying on others while selectively contributing only when convenient.

• **Early Behavioural Problems:** 2 – Childhood aggression, breaking into houses, and early exposure to substances indicate longstanding conduct issues.

• **Lack of Realistic Long-Term Goals:** 2 – Focused on immediate needs, responding reactively rather than planning proactively.

• **Impulsivity:** 2 – Frequent rash decisions, including threats of violence and reckless actions, without regard for consequences.

• **Irresponsibility:** 2 – Repeated failures to meet commitments or obligations, both legal and familial.

• **Juvenile Delinquency:** 2 – Early illegal behaviours included stealing a neighbours car for a joyride, breaking into a vacant house, and early substance use introduced by his stepfather.

- **Adult Antisocial Behaviour:** 2 – Criminal or illegal acts continued into adulthood, including family violence, theft, substance misuse, and reckless driving.

- **Promiscuous Sexual Behaviour:** 0–1 – No evidence of sexual activity outside the observed relationship, though attention-seeking behaviours were noted.

- **Many Short-Term Marital Relationships:** 0–1 – Married once, long-term relationship marked by patterns of sociopathic behaviour impacting relational stability.

Interpretation: Based on these observations, Ex's overall traits align with **high levels of psychopathy, with significant risk of antisocial behaviour and lack of empathy (approximately 31–33/40).** Early trauma, thrill-seeking, repeated manipulation, impulsivity, and minimal empathy create a consistent behavioural pattern across his life.

Why Ex is More Likely a Sociopath Than a Psychopath

When people hear terms like "psychopath" or "sociopath," they often think they're interchangeable—but they aren't. Understanding the difference isn't about labelling someone; it's about noticing patterns, motivations, and the way early experiences shape behaviour. With Ex, the picture is clear: his life, actions, and the way he navigates the world align far more closely with sociopathy than psychopathy.

First, sociopathy is shaped by environment. Early life experiences, family dynamics, trauma, and exposure to harmful influences create a person who learns to survive through manipulation, deception, and sometimes aggression. Ex's upbringing was complicated. From sibling conflict to exposure to illegal substances and early reckless behaviour, his environment didn't nurture careful decision-making or empathy. Instead, it taught him to react, to survive, and to exploit situations to his advantage. Psychopathy, on the other hand, is often innate—a wiring difference in the brain that makes someone naturally detached, calculated, and cold from the start. Ex's behaviour reflects learned survival strategies, not inherent emotional detachment.

Second, relationships reveal a lot. Psychopaths rarely form real bonds—they use people as objects to achieve their goals. Sociopaths, however, can form selective attachments, even if those relationships are messy or harmful. Ex maintains certain connections, for example, the long-term partnership with me, complicated family interactions, and selective alliances, even while repeatedly betraying trust. He's capable of attachment, but it's conditional, fragile, and often used to serve his needs.

Third, consider control and impulsivity. Psychopaths are methodical. They plan, strategise, and manipulate with precision. Ex is the opposite. He acts first, reacts later, and rarely thinks through the long-term consequences. From reckless driving to spur-of-the-moment threats or risky behaviour, his life is a series of impulsive choices. That lack of self-control, combined with thrill-seeking tendencies, screams sociopathy.

Fourth, social influence. Psychopaths are polished, magnetic, and often persuasive—people are drawn to them without realising they're being manipulated. Ex never had that polish. His attempts to influence or assert himself were clumsy, unrefined, and obvious. He inserted himself into conversations, repeated what he'd heard, or made claims without real knowledge. The surface-level talk and erratic behaviour didn't allure; it exposed him.

Finally, there's conscience—or what's left of it. Sociopaths often have a faint moral compass. They might recognise rules, norms, or social consequences but ignore them when convenient. Ex knew when he was doing something "wrong" in society's eyes, yet he repeated harmful actions over and over. Psychopaths rarely recognise moral rules at all—they operate entirely outside empathy or guilt. Ex's selective understanding of right and wrong, mixed with bursts of impulsive behaviour, fits sociopathy perfectly.

In short, Ex's life, behaviours, and coping strategies point squarely toward sociopathy. He is reactive rather than calculated, emotionally inconsistent rather than coldly detached, and socially unpolished rather than manipulative in a sophisticated way. His patterns aren't born—they're learned, honed by experience, environment, and survival instincts.

Understanding this distinction isn't about excusing his behaviour. It's about clarity. Recognising Ex as a sociopath allows us to see his patterns, anticipate risks, and understand the forces driving his choices. It frames the story not as a mystery of inherent evil, but as a cautionary tale of learned behaviours, repeated mistakes, and the enduring impact of early life experiences.

Chapter 6: The Breaking Point

It began the moment he learned about the meeting. Just being told he had to go — the one he had been dreading — was enough to ignite the energy that would ripple through the household for days. His fear didn't look like fear. It was wrapped in anger, a simmering, taut energy that radiated through the walls, the furniture, the air we breathed. My body recognised it instantly: shoulders tensing, stomach tightening, ears tuned to every faint sound.

The micro-aggressions began almost imperceptibly. One evening, I was watching TV, keeping the volume low, trying to sink into quiet, when his legs started kicking periodically against the bed, dressed up like wrestlers leg — up and down, not hitting anyone, but a rhythm that demanded attention. I mirrored it, a tiny, instinctive response, and immediately he reacted: eyes narrowing, a sharp, "What are you doing?" I answered simply, "Mirroring you." And then he did it — the tapping on the bed, fingers drumming, deliberate, testing, trying to provoke a reaction.

I knew the game. After twenty-eight years, you learn the signs, the subtle choreography of manipulation. When I asked a simple question, he'd feign sleep, snoring loudly, and respond in that exaggerated, "What?!" tone as if startled awake. If he were truly asleep, he wouldn't have answered at all. My body stayed alert, posture tight, pulse quickened, every muscle ready to react, even though nothing more happened that night.

The days leading up to the meeting were like this, a slow crescendo of tension. Small gestures, tiny provocations, the atmosphere taut with anticipation. It wasn't violent, not overtly, but it was exhausting — a drain on every nerve, a test of perception, patience, and endurance. Ordinary life continued around us — meals, errands, routines — but underneath, every movement, every sound, was loaded with potential threat.

I noticed everything: the way he shifted in his chair, how his jaw tightened, the slight flinch of his hands on a countertop. I felt it in my own body: stomach knotted, breath shallow, muscles poised to respond. It was a calm that was anything but peaceful, a quiet before the storm, a rehearsal for the crescendo yet to come.

By the night before, the house was steeped in that taut, anticipatory energy. The world outside could have been still, quiet, normal, and yet inside, every heartbeat, every creak of the floorboards, felt magnified. I lay there, listening, waiting, knowing he was playing. Knowing I had to navigate the tension carefully because the real breaking point wasn't just coming from the meeting — it was already simmering in the subtle control, in the quiet manipulation, in the daily micro-battles that left the body tense, the mind alert, and the heart wary.

That night, nothing more happened. No shouting, no confrontation, no escalation. Yet the tension lingered like a shadow, a reminder of how deeply fear, anger, and control could intertwine, and how my body had already been speaking, long before the mind fully understood the storm ahead.

In the days leading up to the meeting, the air itself seemed to tighten. I was witnessing fear disguised as anger, simmering, unpredictable, and always aimed somewhere nearby. He didn't raise his voice, didn't storm through the house. Instead, the manipulation was woven into every gesture, every hesitation, every tiny interaction.

Dinner was a stage of performance and invisibility. I cooked nightly, a ritual that sustained the household, but my labor went unnoticed. And yet, when someone else came over and experienced a well-prepared meal — a holiday roast, a special dessert — he would take over the kitchen, place himself centre stage, as if he did it all the time. Praise poured in, neighbours complimented, relatives admired: "What a wonderful chef!" Behind the curtain, the reality was entirely different. My input was treated as optional, my ideas dismissed before they were even considered. The pathway I envisioned for the garden? Ignored. Suggestions for how the floorboards should be laid? Contradicted, redirected, subtly invalidated. I felt invisible in the very spaces I maintained, my labor erased while he absorbed recognition effortlessly.

Even small micro-incidents piled up, like grains of sand forming a landslide. He tapped his fingers on the side of the bed — a silent provocation. I mirrored the gesture in irritation, and immediately it became a pretext for confrontation. Or so it felt. When I asked him a simple question, he'd answer as though startled awake, a practiced groan, a "what?" that implied I had disturbed him. I knew, after twenty-eight years, that I was being played. My body responded before my mind could name the manipulation — pulse quickened, stomach clenched, muscles braced, ears alert for the next provocation. Even in quiet, the household vibrated with tension.

Outside the house, he was dependable, competent. Fixing neighbours' cars, mowing lawns, helping friends — these acts painted a picture of reliability and generosity. There was a pull there, subtle and strange, but I'd never call it charm. Inside, the same energy was absent when directed toward our family. Requests for participation, even minor ones, became negotiations, tests, or battlegrounds. A mundane task — helping with the girls' school concerts, attending swimming lessons, parent teacher interviews — was rare, or non existent. Public admiration and private indifference formed a quiet but constant backdrop of betrayal.

The manipulation seeped deeper than actions; it infiltrated perception. Did I imagine it? Did I overreact? My mind circled the question, unsure whether reality itself was crooked or if my instincts were lying. Every subtle undermining — a dismissed suggestion, a redirected idea, a silent withdrawal — was a reminder that my body's awareness was more trustworthy than my mind's assessment. The tension between survival instincts and ethical imperatives became almost unbearable. Should I speak up? Should I stay quiet? Each choice carried consequences I had learned to anticipate over decades.

Even kindness was transactional. Small gestures at home — the occasional nod, the rare smile — were always calculated to maintain an image of normalcy or to extract gratitude. The duality was a living thing: magnetism for the outside world, control and indifference at home. My body absorbed it all, a silent witness to the discrepancy, reacting in tension, alertness, and an unspoken readiness for conflict.

By the end of each day, my body told the story my mind could barely articulate. Neck tight, jaw clenched, gut coiled, legs restless — each nerve ending humming with subtle trauma. The accumulation of micro-incidents, the invisible weight of manipulation, the relentless public vs. private disparity — it wasn't just exhausting, it was a form of psychological erosion. I felt myself fray at the edges, yet my instincts remained sharp, sensing every micro-aggression before it landed fully.

This silent tyranny — everyday, invisible, painstakingly deliberate — set the stage for what was inevitable. The cracks, small and almost imperceptible, were widening. The tension, embedded in every interaction, in every gesture, was preparing me, unwittingly, for the breaking point that would demand everything I had learned about reading the body, trusting instincts, and surviving when reason alone wasn't enough.

The days before the breaking point stretched out like taut wires, humming with unspoken threats. Each interaction was a negotiation with invisible landmines. The body knows before the mind does — shoulders stiffen, stomach knots, pulse quickens, blood pressure high. Even the quietest gestures carried menace. He didn't need to raise his voice. A glance, a sudden proximity in the kitchen, a finger tapping impatiently at the edge of a counter — these were enough to trigger that familiar tightening in my chest.

Promises were a currency he never intended to honour. Invitations to engage, to be seen, to rely on him — they dissolved in the daylight. Family events, school concerts, mundane life rituals — milestones I had silently counted on — went unacknowledged. And yet, in the world outside, he was reliable, admired, charming: a man who helped neighbours, fixed cars, presented polished meals at gatherings. The contrast wasn't subtle. It was a sting, daily, like a door closing on expectation. My efforts, my care, my presence — all rendered invisible while his public image soared.

Sometimes overt, sometimes cloaked in menace: "What if I just leave?" "Don't make me call the authorities." Threats of self-harm, of legal action, of punitive consequences for imagined slights — they all carried weight because the body remembers patterns. And I did remember. Some nights were sleepless, ears tuned to the smallest shift: a floorboard creak, a snore that wasn't quite snoring, the slow slide of his footsteps down the hall. My mind raced, asking the impossible question over and over: Am I overreacting? Am I imagining this?

The betrayals compounded in subtle, relentless ways. Requests ignored. Contributions dismissed. Creative ideas undermined. And when I finally did confront him, the gaslighting was immediate: he questioned my memory, my perception, my worth. "That never happened," he would say, voice calm but edged with certainty, and suddenly my recollection felt faulty, my body doubting itself despite the clarity of the moment.

Physical intimidation was present, too — subtle enough to create unease, severe enough to register in the nervous system. Doors slammed, walls pounded, reckless driving with me in the car. Pushed, grabbed, pinched — incidents small enough to be dismissed by others but large enough to leave my body coiled and alert, a constant state of vigilance. Even the pets didn't feel safe; with my dog urinating on his bed, reminders that control extended to everything I loved.

The girls were nearly invisible unless they stumbled, said the wrong thing, or made a noise that drew his irritation. Milestones, small triumphs, ordinary days — all went unacknowledged. Each overlooked moment pressed on me, at times forcing me into both mum and dad roles. I would take my mum, their nan, to Christmas events and concerts, doing everything I could to give my girls the support and celebration they deserved.

And still, he maintained the public persona of generosity and allure. Meals presented, errands completed, friendships nurtured — the careful veneer of a man admired by society. But inside, the household felt like a minefield. Each day, each micro-incident — a subtle put-down, a redirected demand, a sneer disguised as humour — chipped away at sense of safety. My body reacted before my mind could name the betrayal: muscles tense, breath shallow, stomach twisting.

By the time the critical incident arrived, the crescendo had built over months, years, a pattern I had long learned to anticipate but couldn't escape. The betrayal wasn't a single act — it was a symphony of manipulations, threats, gaslighting, invisibility, intimidation, and calculated façade. The body remembered every brushstroke of abuse, every denial, every lie. Every nerve ending was alive, primed for the inevitable collapse.

This crescendo — emotional, physical, psychological — demanded recognition. Not as isolated events, but as a pattern of erosion, a systematic dismantling of trust and safety. The betrayal was total, and in that moment, all the prior micro-incidents coalesced into something undeniable: a reckoning not just with his behaviour, but with the body's insistence on remembering truth when the mind was coerced into doubt.

These patterns weren't new. I had learned, over years of reading his moods, that when anger simmered beneath the surface, the household itself became a fragile, ticking pressure cooker. On those nights, I would move carefully, anticipating the sparks, feeling the weight of his presence even before he spoke. And I found a way — or so I thought — to keep the storm at bay. I would go to him. Entice him. Use sex to calm the tide of tension. Sometimes it was five times a week. My body knew the routine: the slight tremor in my chest, the tightened muscles, the readiness to respond before the chaos began. For the family, for the girls, for the safety of home — I told myself — this was necessary.

But looking back, the truth was stark and sharp. In my desperate attempt to keep peace, I had been feeding the fire. The act that I had believed would calm the house had rewarded his anger, had reinforced the very behaviours that made my gut coil with dread. Every instinct I had learned to trust, every subtle tightening in my shoulders or flicker of unease in my stomach, had been whispering the truth all along. The manipulation wasn't subtle anymore — it was clear, deliberate, undeniable.

It was a slow, creeping realisation, crawling through the fog of self-doubt. Am I imagining this? Am I overreacting? I asked myself these questions again and again, but the answers were in my body — the way my spine stiffened when he entered a room, the racing pulse when he raised his voice, the hollow pit in my stomach when his eyes landed on me with that calculating calm. My instincts were screaming a language I had learned to understand.

And then, in a single quiet moment of reflection, it hit me: I could name it. I could see the pattern — the control, the manipulation, the reward for aggression. I could feel the chains loosen, small but tangible, as awareness replaced confusion. Recognition surged through me like a pulse — a mix of fear and something sharper, something stronger: clarity.

It wasn't a dramatic shift. The household tension didn't vanish, the anger didn't dissolve, and his patterns didn't stop. But inside me, something fundamental had changed.

I could step back. I could witness the manipulation for what it was. I could stop participating, stop feeding it, stop giving my power away. And for the first time in years, I began to choose myself.

My gut, my posture, my instincts — the very sensors I had relied on for survival — were no longer just responses to danger. They were my guide, my compass, pointing me toward agency. The moment of clarity didn't erase the past, but it illuminated a path forward. A way to reclaim my body, my mind, my life. And as terrifying as the insight was, it was also the first spark of freedom I had felt in a long, long time.

Chapter 7: The Reckoning

————

I didn't know, not really, until that day in the course. The Professor (of trauma-informed psychotherapy) wasn't dramatic, not emotional, not trying to shock anyone. He simply said, "If you feel like you're walking on eggshells, that's family violence."

And my body reacted before my mind did.

It felt like the floor inside me gave way. I couldn't breathe for a second — not because of panic, but because something inside me finally spoke the truth I had been swallowing for years. I had always walked on eggshells. Not sometimes. Not occasionally. Always. My whole adult life had been a choreography of hypervigilance. And hearing those words... it was like someone turned on the lights in a room I didn't know I was living in.

It wasn't anxiety. It wasn't "relationship stress." It was violence. And my body had known it long before I let myself admit it.

That moment split my life in two: before awareness and after.

After that course, everything shifted — not in big dramatic scenes, but in the micro-movements of my nervous system. I started noticing myself. My patterns. My body's messages. The way my shoulders tightened when he walked in the room. The way my breath shortened when his voice changed pitch. The way my spine braced when I heard the front door slam. Awareness became a magnifying glass and a mirror.

And as I did the work — the therapy, the self-reflection, the peeling back of denial — something unexpected happened. My innate boundaries started to rise on their own. Boundaries I didn't have to think about or construct. They came up as naturally as flinching from danger.

But boundaries in an unsafe environment aren't just empowering — they're dangerous.

When the girls moved out, the stakes changed. It was just him and me in that house. No buffers. No witnesses. No distractions. I no longer used sex to soothe the aggression or drop his frequency. I wasn't compliant the way I used to be. I withdrew when the energy shifted, protected my space, stayed quiet instead of appeasing.

And every step toward myself — every inch of reclaimed agency — provoked him.

After he spent a month in jail, then another at a caravan park due to the first IVO, he returned to the house. I altered the order so he could come home under strict conditions: no drugs, no family violence, no breaking things, no alcohol around me. I thought he'd changed. He did the courses — anger management, men's behaviour change, drug programs. Three or four of them. He did them the way he did everything: enough to tick the box, enough to look like he was trying.

But the behaviour never stopped. The drugs continued. The volatility simmered. The nice came and went like weather. The drinking wasn't frequent, but the drugs were — the threat lived in the possibility.

It's been a year and a half since he said he would kill me. The words still echo in my bones, stored like an imprint under the skin. And then, the other day, the new threat came: he'd put me through a wall. He'd kick my dog. My body reacted instantly — shaking, gut tight, temperature dropping. A full-system alarm. The kind the mind cannot override. But I've had enough.

I went back to the police station. The IVO I had already extended wasn't strong enough anymore. The police themselves stepped in; they requested it be upgraded to a full IVO, because they believed I was at risk of harm. Hearing that... it was confirmation and terror all at once. I wasn't imagining it. I wasn't overreacting. My body had been right all along.

And all of this was happening while my house was being prepared for sale — the one place that had held all the chaos, all the memories, all the attempts at survival. The fear hit me hard. Could I even find another place to live? Could I afford it? My body, already exhausted, already trembling from years of bracing, was now dealing with survival stress layered with financial fear.

My body — especially my legs and hands — have shaken for years, long before I ever had language for what was happening inside me. The doctor requested I poke out my tongue, stating, "It's not Parkinson's. Your tongue isn't shaking." That was a relief.

A dermatologist once asked me to trim my own toenail so she could check a fungus (gross, I know). My foot was shaking so badly, she was unable to collect the sample.

It was never a mystery illness. It wasn't neurological decline. It wasn't weakness. It was my nervous system, overloaded for decades, firing like a live wire trying to protect me from a threat that lived in my own home.

And I've carried that trembling through everything — motherhood, work, survival, the thousand daily negotiations with danger. The shaking wasn't the start of the collapse. It was the proof that my collapse had been quietly happening for years.

Even now, I work as a therapist — and I'm good at what I do — but I keep my client load small because my body demands it. My emotional capacity is limited, not by talent or passion, but by the sheer volume of vigilance I've lived through. The exhaustion is built into the muscle fibres, into the fascia, into the breath.

And limiting clients means limiting income. And limiting income means the bank won't even consider lending to me. Which leaves me in a brutal equation: whatever I buy next must come from half the sale of the house — because the other half goes to him.

That realisation hit harder than I expected. The fear sat deep, almost primal. After surviving everything — the threats, the volatility, the years of walking on emotional fault lines — the possibility of not being able to rent, not being able to buy, not being able to secure even the most basic safety... it felt like staring into a void.

The fear of homelessness sits on the same shelf as the fear of violence in the nervous system. Both feel like obliteration. Both activate the same alarms.

So here I am, handling client appointments, responding to real estate calls — all the external signs of "normal life" — while inside my body is still vibrating with a history it hasn't yet laid down. The shaking hasn't vanished yet, but now I understand why it's there. And I hold onto the hope that separation from him will give my nervous system the first real chance it's ever had to settle.

For years, the trembling felt like a flaw. Now, it feels like truth. Not weakness, not failure — but the body's record of surviving too much for too long.

And this... this is the breaking point that isn't a collapse so much as a reckoning. A moment where I stop pretending. A moment where the cost of endurance becomes undeniable. A moment where I choose myself, even with body shakes.

The breaking point was never a single explosion. It was the slow accumulation of tremors, the thousand micro-fractures that finally split open. And when it came, it wasn't chaos — it was clarity. My body, trembling and insistent, became the narrator of truth I could no longer deny.

This was *The Breaking Point*: the moment survival stopped being enough, the moment endurance demanded transformation. It was the line between silence and recognition, between shrinking and reclaiming space. My body had carried the record of every threat, every manipulation, every night of vigilance — and now it demanded I listen. The shakes were not weakness. They were testimony. They were the drumbeat of a life that could no longer be contained.

Even as I began to reclaim agency, the tremors persisted. They were stubborn, visceral reminders of a nervous system that had been engaged in prolonged hypervigilance. But their meaning shifted. Once alarms of imminent threat, they became signals of awareness, proof of survival. Each pulse, each quiver, was information about how my body had processed decades of danger. Listening to these signals became a practice of intelligence — of body wisdom, of honouring the lived experience of endurance.

I realised that survival had never been the end goal. Survival had been the foundation — a necessary, instinctive response to years of unpredictability and control. The true work began when survival met awareness, when the body's signals could be interpreted and acted upon with intentionality. Tremors, tension, hypervigilance — these became teachers, not shackles. They were data points, guiding me toward safety, agency, and authenticity.

Through this embodied work, boundaries emerged organically. I no longer needed to negotiate my presence through appeasement or fear. Small acts of assertion — a pause in conversation, a refusal to participate in escalation, a silent withdrawal from provocation — were acts of reclaiming autonomy. The body's tremors were no longer a liability; they were a language, a system of intelligence that had been speaking for decades, waiting for recognition.

Even external markers of progress — upgraded IVOs, legal protections, the sale of the house, and the logistical steps toward independence — were less about action and more about alignment between body, mind, and environment. Safety wasn't granted by documents or systems alone; it was anchored in my own nervous system. The body, once overwhelmed, now carried the authority of presence.

This reclamation wasn't instantaneous or linear. Each day required attention, practice, and patience. Each tremor reminded me of a system that had survived extraordinary stress, and each conscious breath reinforced a capacity for embodied choice. Over time, the accumulation of micro-acts — pausing, observing, breathing, asserting, moving deliberately — generated macro-change: the ability to navigate relationships, spaces, and threats with grounded awareness, authenticity, and authority.

By integrating awareness, body intelligence, and practical boundaries, I finally experienced the first true sense of internal alignment. The body's language — tremors, tension, pulse — was no longer a record of victimhood but a guide toward wholeness. Survival was no longer reactive; it had become strategic, conscious, and intentional. Each day, each movement, each recognition of bodily intelligence was a step toward freedom, toward reclaiming power, toward living fully embodied, fully awake, fully myself.

Awareness created ripples that touched every aspect of life. Simple gestures — breathing fully, adjusting posture, slowing movements — became rituals of reclamation. Every micro-intervention reinforced a new baseline, a subtle re-calibration of the nervous system. The tremors didn't disappear overnight, but they shifted in meaning: once proof of constant threat, now markers of sur-vival, presence, and the wisdom carried in the body.

I began to notice that the old hypervigilance was less rigid. Where previously my body reacted automatically, now it could assess: is this danger real, or is this a memory of past threat? The nervous system began to differentiate between historical echoes and present reality, allowing a form of freedom I had never known. My body was no longer a hostage to fear; it was an instrument of in-sight.

Interactions with him became exercises in observation and boundary-setting. Words that previously triggered panic or compliance were met with calm awareness. I recognised manipulative patterns — provocations, gaslighting, presence — and chose not to participate. Silence became a tool. Stillness be-came a form of resistance. The body, attuned to danger for decades, could now guide measured action rather than frantic reaction. I was finally reading my own internal signals with clarity, trusting my gut where once it had been drowned out by doubt and denial.

This shift extended beyond confrontation. Everyday life began to feel different: the house felt lighter, despite lingering memories. Decisions, once fraught with the tension of negotiation and survival, became deliberate and grounded. Au-tonomy wasn't a theory; it was a lived, tactile experience. My hands, trembling for years, now carried both caution and power. My spine, once braced against unseen threats, began to lengthen in recognition of safety. My breath, formerly shallow and controlled by alertness, expanded with quiet confidence.

Parenting shifted in a way I didn't expect. My daughters weren't looking at me with admiration for staying — they were looking at me with confusion, trying to understand why their mother, the strong one, the steady one, remained in something that hurt her. It was fear that kept me there — fear of losing financial stability, of becoming homeless, of having to start over. All the years of fighting tooth and nail to own our home, only to imagine starting from scratch, made the thought almost unbearable.

The truth is, I'm grateful they don't understand. Their inability to comprehend staying means they haven't internalised the warped logic that abuse teaches you. It means their nervous systems never learned to normalise danger the way mine once did. They lived in the storm, yes, but they didn't absorb the script.

And maybe — just maybe — that's where generational abuse ends. Maybe the thread was already fraying years ago when they were little and I told them, "You don't have to play with anyone who isn't nice to you." A simple sentence at the time, but now I see it for what it was: the first seed of discernment, the first whisper of boundaries, the first quiet rebellion against everything I was still trying to survive.

Socially, the world began to feel navigable again. I could participate in events, conversations, and obligations without carrying the weight of constant vigilance. External pressure or influence no longer dictated my internal state. The nervous system, once a recorder of every slight, now acted as a barometer, differentiating between real threat and habitual echoes. My interactions, previously filtered through anxiety and tension, became clearer, more intentional.

Therapeutically, I saw the threads of embodied trauma weaving through years of work with clients. I recognised patterns in their nervous systems similar to my own: tremors, tension, hypervigilance, subtle signs of chronic survival mode. My lived experience became a lens through which I could guide others, teaching them to observe, interpret, and reclaim their bodily intelligence. The nervous system, long a silent narrator, could be read, understood, and harnessed as a guide to authentic life.

The acts of recognition, of noticing micro-shifts in my body, created momentum. Each breath, each pause, each conscious acknowledgment of tension or tremor became a small victory. Over time, these small victories coalesced into a new equilibrium: a nervous system that could experience safety, that could respond to stress without collapsing into hypervigilance, that could hold agency even amidst uncertainty.

What had once felt like endless chaos — the constant vigilance, the tremors, the micro-aggressions, the manipulation — now had a narrative arc. The body, which had borne witness silently for decades, had become both recorder and teacher. Survival gave way to agency. Fear gave way to clarity. Tremors, once interpreted as weakness, now marked endurance — proof that a life that had survived the unthinkable could assert itself.

This recognition, slow and embodied, marked the transition from surviving to choosing. The nervous system, formerly a battleground, had become a guide and compass of wisdom. And within that shift, the breaking point transformed into something profoundly different: not collapse, not surrender, not chaos — but clarity, agency, and the first real taste of unmediated freedom.

The body doesn't lie. It remembers every betrayal, every manipulation, every shadow of threat, long after the mind has tried to rationalise, dismiss, or forget. My nervous system carried decades of subtle assaults like a score of music written in tension and tremors, and now it was beginning to play a new composition: one of awareness, presence, and self-sovereignty. Every micro-movement — the shift of weight in a chair, the tightening of a jaw, the flutter of fingers — became a whisper of truth I could finally hear.

And that is the essence of *The Breaking Point*: not the collapse itself, but the reclamation that follows. The moment when survival becomes agency, when tremors become testimony, when the body's language is finally heard as truth. It is the point where endurance transforms into clarity, where vigilance reshapes into freedom, where the body, after decades of carrying danger, begins to carry dignity instead.

Chapter 8: The Awakening

———

It takes time to realise that manipulation is not chaos. That what feels like random cruelty, sudden outbursts, or emotional turbulence is often highly orchestrated. Once clarity settles in, the patterns emerge, and with them comes the uncomfortable, almost clinical understanding: this behaviour is deliberate.

In public, the world often sees magnetism, a carefully constructed persona. There was no humour for the crowd, no easy warmth — only a quiet aloofness, a magnetic pull reserved for those inside his sphere, masking the undercurrent beneath. But behind closed doors, the rules were different. The allure evaporated. Control, intimidation, subtle punishments — these became the tools of daily interaction. The contrast is not accidental. It is strategic. It is designed to maintain dominance, to keep the other person off balance, to create a quiet dependency that is almost invisible from the outside.

I began to notice the cycles: moments of reward followed by punishment. Praise and approval when I acquiesced, coldness and silence when I asserted myself. The tiny victories of compliance were reinforced, the smallest resistances punished. It is a rhythm that rewires perception. It exploits our natural desire to connect, to belong, to be seen and valued. Empathy, patience, and even intuition — traits that make us human — become vulnerabilities in this context.

Manipulation is rarely loud. It whispers. It erodes confidence incrementally. It invites doubt at exactly the points where trust should be strongest: in relationships, in the self, in the home you call safe. You start questioning your own instincts. "Am I reading too much into this?" "Is it all in my head?" "Could I be mistaken?" The erosion is slow, almost imperceptible, until suddenly you realise that your own body, your own judgment, has been bending under the weight of someone else's engineered control.

For me, recognition came in moments that were both ordinary and extraordinary. The small inconsistencies, the subtle gaslighting, the invisible reordering of reality. One day, it was a contradiction in a story — something he said yesterday didn't match the version today. My gut tensed. My spine stiffened. The mind raced: was this normal forgetfulness, or was it deliberate? And slowly, almost painfully, the answer revealed itself. Deliberate. Designed. Calculated.

Manipulative people operate like this because it works. There is power in unpredictability, in the ability to destabilise another person while maintaining the appearance of normalcy. The aura in public isn't generosity; it is a tool to maintain reputation, to disarm potential witnesses, to create a buffer against accountability. The control in private is the laboratory of influence, where the dynamics of obedience, fear, and dependence are tested and perfected. It is not personal — at least, not in the way we feel it. It is tactical.

Yet, even as we understand the mechanics, the effect on the human psyche is profound. Empathy becomes a double-edged sword. Trust becomes a liability. Self-doubt grows like a vine, wrapping itself around decisions, emotions, and reactions. You start living in a state of second-guessing, measuring yourself against an invisible standard set by someone whose goal is not connection but control. The subtlety is key. Too much aggression would trigger intervention, suspicion, or escape. The manipulation must be invisible enough that you don't see it until the pattern is so embedded that recognition feels destabilising, almost shocking.

I can remember a dozen moments that illustrate this perfectly. The praise for a minor concession, the cold shoulder for asking a simple question, the contradictory statements that left me questioning my memory. Each one, on its own, seemed minor. On its own, it could be dismissed. But stacked together, repeated over months and years, the architecture of influence became undeniable. It was a system designed to undermine my autonomy, to make me doubt my own instincts, to create reliance on his interpretation of reality.

And therein lies the cruel genius of manipulation: it exploits human nature. The desire to be seen, to be understood, to be valued — all of it is used against you. Moments of kindness become rewards, compliance becomes conditioned, rebellion triggers repercussion. It's a quiet, invisible rhythm, one that is exhausting precisely because it is almost imperceptible. It is not wild rage or predictable aggression. It is subtle, insidious, and terrifyingly effective.

Understanding this does not erase the pain. It does not retroactively undo the anxiety, the trembling, the slow depletion of trust in oneself. But it provides a map. It illuminates why certain reactions are so visceral, why certain interactions make the nervous system tighten, why your mind struggles to trust what it once took for granted. Recognition becomes the first step toward reclaiming authority over your own body, your own perception, your own decisions.

There is also a strange relief in understanding. Once you see the mechanism, once you can identify the rhythm and logic of manipulation, the terror loses some of its power. It doesn't vanish — you are still navigating a dangerous terrain — but the map exists now, and maps give agency. You can anticipate, predict, and protect. You can begin to respond rather than react. And perhaps most importantly, you can separate your sense of self from the manipulator's design. The blame, the shame, the self-doubt — none of it was yours to carry.

I remember one night vividly. I was processing a series of interactions that had left me feeling exhausted and unsure. As I traced the sequence, I realised something startling: I could see the pattern before it unfolded. The reward would follow compliance, the silence would follow assertion, the charm would appear in public while control tightened in private. And in that realisation came a quiet, powerful shift. My body no longer needed to react immediately. My mind could measure, assess, and prepare. Awareness had created a buffer between stimulus and response — a sliver of freedom I had not known for years.

This is the paradox of manipulation: it is profoundly human and yet profoundly destructive. It leverages the very traits that connect us — empathy, trust, care — and turns them into mechanisms of control. It is deeply personal and yet methodically engineered. And yet, by recognising its structure, by understanding its cycles and its purpose, we reclaim power. Knowledge becomes armour. Awareness becomes strategy. Recognition becomes freedom.

To this day, I reflect on the duality constantly. People can be dazzling, magnetic, funny, warm — and still wield control with calculated precision behind closed doors. The public performance and the private reality are two sides of the same coin, and awareness of that duality is critical. It is the lens through which we understand the manipulator and, more importantly, understand how to maintain our own boundaries, trust our instincts, and honour our own nervous system's wisdom.

This understanding — clinical, reflective, precise — is what allows hope to exist in a grounded way. Because once you know the patterns, once you see the design, you can chart a course that preserves your autonomy, your dignity, and your sense of self. You don't have to absorb the manipulation. You don't have to internalise it. You can navigate it, respond to it, and eventually move beyond it. Awareness transforms experience into insight. Insight transforms fear into strategy. And strategy, eventually, transforms survival into choice.

There is a subtlety to manipulation that most people don't see until it's already embedded. Manipulative personalities do not operate randomly. They are methodical, precise, and attentive, scanning for vulnerabilities like a radar tuned to need, insecurity, and self-doubt. Understanding who they target is not about assigning blame—it's about illumination, awareness, and ultimately, self-protection.

Those who have lived with histories of rejection or abandonment often carry a silent, invisible scar. Early experiences of being overlooked, dismissed, or unloved create an unspoken hunger for recognition. This is not weakness—it is human. We are wired for connection. But manipulators sense this need, and their calculated personas are designed to activate it. They offer attention, smiles, and praise, not freely but as currency. Approval becomes conditional, earned through compliance, and their manufactured presence draws the vulnerable into a web that feels intimate, affirming, and ultimately dangerous. The hook is subtle: the warmth is real enough to feel rewarding, but it is never consistent, never unconditional. Over time, the longing for connection strengthens the grip, and the line between genuine care and engineered manipulation blurs.

Manipulators are keen observers, often reading far more than words. They notice the subtle signals that reveal who is open to influence: a slight slump in posture, a hesitant glance, the way someone offers reassurance before it's even asked for. They see the tension in shoulders, the quick nods of agreement, the softening of the voice when unsure. These are not weaknesses—they are human, natural responses—but to a calculated persona, they are invitations. Awareness of how one presents outwardly is the first step toward protecting the internal world.

Manipulative personalities are keenly attuned to the signals people unconsciously broadcast through words, tone, and behaviour. They notice those who apologise excessively, even when no harm has been done, or those who defer constantly, asking, "Is it okay if...?" before taking the simplest action. They pick up on the repeated minimisation of needs: "I don't want to be a burden," "It's fine," or "I'm just being too sensitive." These phrases reveal a person's tendency to prioritise others' feelings above their own, to question their own perceptions, or to assume responsibility for outcomes that aren't theirs. Even subtle verbal cues — the hesitant tone, over-explaining, softening statements with qualifiers — signal an openness, a lack of overt caution that can make someone more approachable to a calculated persona. Manipulators also scan for patterns of over-commitment or self-sacrifice, listening for individuals who regularly prioritise everyone else's needs, who defer their own desires, or who replay learned family dynamics through guilt and excessive people-pleasing. They sense vulnerability in the gaps between words and presence — the tension in a voice, the softening of facial expressions, the pauses before speaking, the eagerness to reassure or seek approval. These are not weaknesses, but human behaviours, natural and often invisible to the person carrying them. Yet to someone who is attuned to influence, they are invitations, clear markers of potential prey. Recognising these cues is essential: when we notice what we broadcast externally — the words we choose, the hesitations in our speech, the ways we apologise or explain ourselves — we can begin to reclaim the subtle control we unknowingly surrender, turning awareness into a quiet form of resilience and self-protection.

Empathetic and trusting personalities are also frequent targets. Empathy is a superpower—it allows us to feel, understand, and respond to the needs of others. But in the presence of someone with a calculated façade, empathy can become a vulnerability. Manipulators understand the mechanics of forgiveness and rationalisation. They know that empathetic individuals will often assume responsibility for another's emotional state, will excuse behaviour that is inconsistent, and will offer second chances long before the offender earns them. This is not naïveté; it is a willingness to see the good in others, to hope for harmony, to believe in redemption. It is a strength, yet it becomes a lever that manipulators pull with precision.

Conflict-averse individuals are particularly susceptible. People who fear confrontation or prioritise harmony over personal needs often find themselves caught in cycles of appeasement. Manipulators escalate tension in subtle ways, observing responses, and adjusting pressure until the victim yields. What may begin as minor discomfort—an awkward word, a shift in tone, a small demand—escalates incrementally until the internal cost is exhaustion. Compliance feels safer than confrontation, but every act of appeasement reinforces the manipulator's control, strengthening the pattern of conditional safety. Over time, avoidance becomes a coping mechanism that feeds the cycle, leaving the victim unsure of their boundaries and increasingly reliant on external validation.

The sense of duty that guides their decisions is powerful and noble, yet manipulators exploit it systematically. A parent may be willing to sacrifice personal comfort to maintain stability for children, a partner may suppress intuition to maintain peace, a caretaker may overlook their own needs for the apparent good of someone else. Manipulators perceive these tendencies and tailor their behaviour accordingly. They know that threats, emotional withdrawal, or subtle pressure will trigger the caregiver's instinct to protect and provide, even when the environment is unsafe. In such dynamics, love and responsibility are weaponised—not maliciously by the caregiver, but strategically by the manipulator.

When a person doubts their own perceptions, questions their instincts, or carries a sense of being "not enough," they are highly susceptible to gaslighting. Manipulators exploit this predisposition, planting doubt in subtle, almost imperceptible ways. A dismissive comment becomes a pattern of disorientation, a small inconsistency becomes evidence that the victim's memory is unreliable, and over time, the individual begins to question their reality. The manipulator's power thrives in this gap between perception and trust in self. Yet, these patterns are not permanent; the body, mind, and intuition carry signals of mis-alignment long before the mind fully comprehends the manipulation.

Recognising these vulnerabilities is not about self-blame—it is about reclaiming awareness. A person who has been overlooked, empathetic, conflict-averse, responsible, or insecure does not invite manipulation through their humanity. They are operating with the strengths that make life meaningful and relationships rich. The manipulator is not responding to a flaw—they are exploiting access points in human complexity that exist in all of us. Understanding this difference is empowering: it shifts the lens from shame to insight, from self-criticism to strategy, from victimhood to grounded awareness.

The subtlety of the manipulator's approach is key. They rarely rely on overt aggression; instead, they calibrate responses, observe reactions, and apply pressure with a rhythm designed to foster dependence. Their calculated personas are tailored for the audience—the orchestrated likability, the engineered persona, the polished performance. To outsiders, they may radiate magnetism, gravitas, or presence. There is a pull, often quiet, that compels attention and creates trust. But for those within the inner circle, the effect is different: the warmth is conditional, the humour measured, and the kindness instrumented. It is in the private interactions, the micro-moments, the decisions made behind closed doors, where their true nature surfaces.

Empathetic people may initially rationalise these discrepancies: "They're just having a bad day," "It's stress," or "Maybe I misunderstood." Over time, however, the repetition of subtle manipulations—dismissals, emotional unavailability, selective praise—erodes confidence. Conflict-averse individuals may continue to appease, caregivers may overextend, and those with fragile self-worth may internalise blame. The manipulator thrives on this feedback loop, fine-tuning behaviour to maintain influence while maintaining the illusion of charm. It is methodical, calculated, and highly effective.

Understanding these dynamics offers a dual opportunity: to recognise patterns in oneself and to recognise them in others. Awareness is not merely intellectual; it is also embodied. A tightening in the stomach, a racing heartbeat, or sudden doubt can be signals of misalignment. The body senses subtle threats even when the mind rationalises them away. Trusting these internal cues is a form of resilience. By observing reactions, setting gentle boundaries, and acknowledging personal needs, individuals can develop internal markers of safety. They can learn to differentiate between genuine care and conditional attention, between empathy and exploitation, between support and manipulation.

Examples from real life illustrate these principles clearly. The friend who only calls when they need advice exploits generosity; the partner whose apologies come only after confrontation manipulates conflict-averse tendencies; the colleague who offers praise selectively uses insecurity as a lever. Each instance carries patterns that are recognisable once seen, and each is an opportunity to strengthen personal awareness. Over time, recognising these patterns builds confidence and restores agency without eroding empathy. Awareness allows for connection without compromise of integrity.

In practice, developing awareness requires self-reflection and support. Journaling interactions, noting emotional and physical responses, and consulting trusted advisors or therapists can reveal cycles that were previously invisible. Small steps—pausing before responding, observing rather than reacting, reaffirming personal values—create a scaffold for emotional and psychological resilience. Over time, these practices reinforce a sense of internal stability, reducing susceptibility to external influence while maintaining the capacity for care, connection, and trust.

Manipulative individuals will often continue to seek access, testing limits and probing for openings. Yet the clearer the boundaries and the stronger the internal compass, the less effective their strategies become. Recognising vulnerability does not erase it, but it allows one to engage with intention rather than reflex. Where once there may have been self-doubt or internalised blame, there is now observation, discernment, and strength. Where once there may have been confusion, there is now clarity and grounded hope. The shift is subtle but profound: from being a target to understanding the mechanisms of influence, from reactive to informed, from disempowered to aware.

This understanding is the foundation of healing. It is not about erasing sensitivity, empathy, or responsibility—it is about honouring these traits while pro tecting one's own well-being. The process requires courage: to see the truth, to accept the impact of exploitation, and to make choices that support long-term resilience. It is a gradual realignment, a recalibration of both perception and self-worth, anchored in the recognition that strength does not require abandoning humanity. On the contrary, it flourishes through awareness, care, and intentionality.

In the end, recognising who manipulators prey upon is a gift of insight. It allows one to navigate relationships with eyes open, to honour personal limits, and to cultivate environments of support rather than exploitation. Those who have been vulnerable in the past can reclaim power not through force or retaliation, but through knowledge, grounded action, and trust in their own intuition. Awareness does not make the pull of calculated personas vanish—but it provides the tools to respond with clarity, presence, and hope. It is the first step toward living with courage and connecting authentically, without losing oneself in the process.

As I began to work deeply on myself — particularly at a subconscious level through hypnotherapy — I noticed something profound: the more I resolved the internal conflicts and dissolved the old patterns in my system, the more my boundaries began to assert themselves naturally. It wasn't a conscious effort at first; it felt like my body was remembering what it had always known but had been trained to ignore. The distance I created between myself and his energy — that controlling, unpredictable frequency — allowed me to notice what I would tolerate and what I wouldn't.

Before this work, I had tried constantly to "fix" the dynamic, to restore some semblance of connection. I would approach him, trying to resolve arguments, attempting to negotiate peace, often breaking down in tears. It wasn't truly connection — the kind that flows both ways, that is felt and returned — it was a desperate attempt to extract from him something my system longed for but never received. There were moments of relief afterward, often in quiet tears, and a slow, creeping awareness that the fear of him leaving wasn't as gripping as it had been.

As my internal strength grew, my choices began to reflect it. I started prioritising myself in small, tangible ways. Cooking became a clear marker: I prepared meals for my own health and enjoyment, not to appease him. If he didn't like what I made, he could feed himself — that was his responsibility. Setting that boundary wasn't just about food; it was a statement of self-respect, a refusal to sacrifice my needs for his comfort.

Other boundaries were far more personal, far more intimate. I had to repeatedly tell him not to touch me without consent — an act that should never have needed repetition. Each time I said, "I don't like it," I faced resistance, silent treatment, or escalation. Change didn't happen instantly; it required patience, courage, and repetition. Each time I stood firm, my nervous system registered a quiet victory — a shift from compliance born of fear to presence born of choice.

The exhaustion was real. Exhaustion from the constant need to assert, to reinforce, to survive in a space where my consent had never been respected. And yet, in these small acts — leaving the bedroom when boundaries were crossed, standing firm on what was acceptable, cooking only for myself — there was relief. My posture relaxed, my breath deepened, and I began to experience moments of ease that had once been impossible.

Even behaviours that once drained me, like the tapping, fake snoring, or small irritations meant to provoke, no longer held the same power. My body had learned to protect itself, to quiet external chaos in order to preserve internal calm. And in those moments, I could see clearly: a boundary is only meaningful if it is maintained consistently. When I left the room, refusing to negotiate my personal space, I wasn't being dramatic or punitive; I was sending a signal that my limits mattered, that my body, my presence, demanded respect. Eventually, those signals were received, sometimes halting behaviours entirely.

I also began to understand the mechanics of manipulation on a deeper level. What can seem subconscious — the kicking, tapping, mock snoring — is often entirely justified in the manipulator's mind. They rationalise, "I had no choice" or "They deserved it," creating a reality where their actions feel reasonable. The trick is that when you begin asserting boundaries, you challenge not just behaviour but the very narrative that supports it. That's why the small victories — a refusal, a pause, a step back — are monumental. Each one rewires your nervous system, recalibrates the body, and quietly shifts the power dynamic.

Through this process, I discovered the courage in repetition and the strength in subtlety. Autonomy isn't always dramatic. Sometimes, it's cooking for yourself, claiming your space in silence, asserting consent over and over, until your body finally believes it belongs to you. These incremental acts — grounded in posture, breath, presence, and persistence — became the foundation for self-trust. Each one reminded me that my safety, my voice, and my needs were non-negotiable, and that even the smallest assertion can ripple outward into profound internal authority.

Even as the chapter draws to a close, the lessons are subtle, lived, and bodily — not just intellectual. Awareness, boundaries, agency, self-trust — these aren't milestones marked with fanfare; they accumulate quietly, in breath, in posture, in the firmness of saying "no," in the decision to step away when personal space is violated. Each act, however small, carries weight. Each refusal, each insistence on consent, each moment prioritising my own needs over the expectations of another rewired my system. The nervous system began to learn what safety felt like, what respect looked like, and what autonomy could feel like when allowed to breathe. Resilience is not the absence of struggle; it is the quiet, persistent reclaiming of power, moment by moment, until confidence is no longer borrowed from others but lived in the body itself.

There is also humility in this process. None of it happens in isolation. Support — even minimal — shapes possibility. I could not have stepped into this freedom without the guidance and protection offered by external allies, like the police ensuring my safety, or the structural safeguard of an IVO in place. These small scaffolds of security allowed me to begin the larger work of reclaiming myself. And as I exercised agency in tangible ways — deciding what to eat, where to spend my time, who to allow into my inner world — I discovered the profound joy of choice, of ownership over life that had long felt dictated by another's frequency.

The lessons I carry now are universal. Everyone has overlooked instincts, deferred to fear, or ignored the quiet signals the body sends. We have all, at times, prioritised someone else's needs above our own, questioned our perceptions, or felt the subtle pull of manipulation and dismissed it. Recognising this is not shameful; it is human. Awareness itself is a gift. When we notice the patterns of control, when we name the moments where our autonomy was subtly eroded, we gain the power to respond differently — to reclaim our presence, our voice, and our sense of self.

Where have you ignored your instincts? What small acts of agency have you overlooked, dismissed, or deferred? Reflection is not merely an intellectual exercise; it is a bodily practice. A tense shoulder, a quickened heartbeat, a hesitant glance — these are signals of misalignment, nudges from a system designed to protect you. Each acknowledgment, each conscious act of self-honour, reinforces the internal compass, making it clearer, stronger, and more trustworthy.

Looking forward, life need not be monumental to be extraordinary. For me, this means small freedoms: choosing to cook for myself, creating meals that nourish rather than placate, stepping into spaces that feel expansive and light rather than confined. It means embracing work that is joy, that gives energy rather than drains it. It means imagining daily life as a holiday, allowing each day to hold its own richness, and giving myself permission to breathe fully into it. These acts, small and deliberate, are the architecture of resilience, the embodiment of self-trust, and the quiet reclamation of agency.

And as I take these steps, I feel it most in the body: a deep exhale, a chest that lifts, shoulders that relax, a spine that straightens not in defiance, but in alignment with self. It is a sunrise that begins in the nervous system, in awareness, in presence. A quiet signal that says: you are here. You belong. You are capable. Freedom is not a distant horizon — it is already in the sensations, in the choices, in the clarity you are learning to honour. And in that presence, the journey becomes not only survivable, but luminous, grounded, and wholly your own.

There is a particular kind of danger that lives in a sociopath when their grip begins to loosen—an atmosphere, not an action. It shifts the air. Thickens it. You feel it before you understand it. A storm gathering behind their eyes, silent at first, then swelling into something unpredictable, something that makes your body go rigid with ancient knowing: *stay alert... anything could erupt.*

People often imagine sociopaths as loud, violent, explosive. But the truth is more unnerving.

The real danger arrives when they feel control slipping from their fingers—not gradually, but like sand they thought they owned. And in that moment, they don't just panic. They retaliate with whatever they believe will restore their power.

Sometimes that's rage.

Sometimes it's threats.

Sometimes it's a sudden, chilling silence.

And sometimes it's something far more disturbing—weaponised despair, declarations of self-harm, or suicidal threats designed not from pain, but precision.

For twenty-eight years, I watched this cycle play out in subtle patterns and catastrophic ruptures. When he lost control, he didn't collapse. He *strategised*. His nervous system was wired for domination, not connection; for leverage, not love. And every emotional display was a calculated move to pull the spotlight back onto himself.

When he felt cornered—financially, emotionally, or socially—the shift was instant. Eyes would glaze, jaw would tighten, and suddenly he'd talk about how "there was no point anymore," or how "everyone would be better off without him."

Words designed to twist my insides.

Words meant to force compliance.

Words meant to remind me that my safety, my children's safety, and even his own life were all somehow my responsibility.

Science shows that individuals with high antisocial traits often use **crisis language** as a manipulation tactic rather than an expression of genuine intent.[1] They are drawn not to relief, but to **reaction**—your reaction. Your panic. Your attempts to soothe. Your willingness to abandon boundaries you were finally brave enough to set.

I learned quickly that when he threatened self-destruction, what he was really saying was:

"Give me control back."

"Don't pull away."

"Don't choose yourself."

It wasn't vulnerability. It was a weapon.

The irony?

While the world sees suicidal threats as a cry for help, living with him taught me to see it as a **cry for dominance**—a last attempt to anchor himself into the centre of the room, the centre of the narrative, the centre of my fear.

There were nights where he disappeared for hours, returning with the scent of chaos on him—drugs, deceit, and stories crafted to keep me guessing. When I asked where he had been, he'd shrug or smirk or turn it back onto me: *"Why does it matter?"*

Because I was the one keeping the family afloat.

Because I was the one counting coins in envelopes hidden behind books.

Because I was the one picking up the emotional debris he created.

But each time I stood up to him, even quietly, even gently, he would lean into the chaos.

Not physically violent—psychologically volatile.

It was his favourite battlefield.

And my body felt it first.

The freeze response. The shallow breath. The racing heart.

My bio-intelligence knew I was in danger long before my mind pieced it together.

Losing control does something particular to a sociopath:

it fractures their illusion of superiority.

And when their self-image is threatened, they often reach for the most dramatic, destabilising tools they can find to pull the emotional centre of gravity back toward them.

Threats of self-harm.

Statements about ending it all.

Dark proclamations whispered like ultimatums.

Not because they want to die—but because they want you to surrender.

These moments aren't just frightening.

They are disorienting.

They're designed to be.

Because a confused partner is an easier partner to control.

I remember standing in the kitchen once, hands shaking, as he spiralled into one of these theatrical collapses. My girls were asleep. The house was quiet. And every instinct in me knew the danger wasn't in what he might do to himself—it was in what he might do to *us* emotionally if I didn't fold.

People assume that leaving someone like him is the final battle.

But the truth?

The most dangerous version of him existed in the days he realised I no longer feared him.

The nights he sensed he was losing access to my mind.

The moments my boundaries stopped trembling.

It wasn't his anger that terrified me.

It was his despair—because that's where his cruelty sharpened.

The danger wasn't the threat itself.

The danger was the **intent** behind it.

Living with a sociopath taught me that when control slips, they don't fall apart—they recruit you to hold them together, using guilt, fear, or emotional brinkmanship to pull you back into the role they chose for you.

But what he didn't know was this:

My nervous system was recalibrating.

My awareness was strengthening.

My sense of self was rising quietly beneath the fear.

And eventually, his threats lost their power.

The spell broke.

My body stopped responding in compliance and started responding in truth.

That's the moment he became the most dangerous—and the moment I became the most free.

Chapter 9: The Cost of Hope

———

I don't think people truly understand the kind of hope a woman can hold when she believes — with every fibre of her body's ancient wiring — that love can be repaired if she just tries hard enough. That if she leans in, shows up, softens, carries more, forgives more, sacrifices more... maybe, finally, the chaos will settle. Maybe she'll be safe. Maybe she'll be chosen.

I lived in that hope for years.

And I didn't hope passively. I worked for it. I pushed for it. I carried it. I invested thousands of dollars, thousands of hours, and thousands of micro-moments of emotional labour into trying to get us somewhere better — somewhere stable, somewhere kind, somewhere human.

One of our biggest efforts was the endless car projects. Thousands poured into rebuilding, restoring, replacing. I thought if he had something meaningful to focus on, something mechanical to channel his attention into, maybe he'd put down the marijuana. Maybe engaging his hands would quiet the internal storms. Maybe the routine, the structure, the concentration would help his nervous system recalibrate.

That was the dream: that the cars would save him.

But cars don't heal trauma. Steel and bolts don't replace therapy. Engines don't untangle neurological wiring carved by violence, neglect, or chaos. So even as the projects grew, so did the patterns — the shutdowns, the anger, the withdrawal, the avoidance, the spirals. And I kept trying anyway.

The more I learned in my profession, the harder I tried at home. Stories, metaphors, gentle nudges, subtle invitations to healing. I held onto this wild hope that if I could just find the right doorway into his inner world, I could inspire him toward change. I could guide him to the softness he deserved. I truly believed that if I could understand him deeply enough, I could help him understand himself.

I was doing therapy around him, beside him, through him — without ever calling it therapy.

I sent him to therapists. Multiple. And each time, I carried this quiet belief: "Maybe this is the one. Maybe this is the moment something cracks open."

The first therapist re-traumatised him.

The second therapist, unbelievably, used the very first appointment to urge him to press charges against the uncle who molested him — paperwork and pen ready on the desk. No safety. No pacing. No understanding of his nervous system's fragility. No awareness of how abrupt confrontation can shatter someone already hanging on by a thread. That appointment slammed a door shut before it even opened.

The third therapist... well, she hardly existed. Cancelled sessions. Rescheduled sessions. No-shows where he'd turn up and sit there waiting for someone who simply didn't come. And even when she did show up, all they seemed to do was talk — talk around, talk about, talk through — never getting close to the core, never guiding him inward, never touching the deeper structure of change.

It was crushing. Every time. Absolutely crushing.

Because with every appointment, I silently carried the hope that *this time* he'd choose change. *This time* something would shift. *This time* I'd finally see the man he could have been standing at the doorway.

But here's the truth I kept avoiding: a therapist can only help a client who wants to change.

There's a common saying in the therapy world: "How many therapists does it take to change a light bulb? Only one — but the light bulb has to want to change."

And that was us. That was him. That was the brutal, immovable heart of the matter.

I tried everything. I tried communication tools — "I feel" statements — only to be met with eye rolls, silence, or that empty, blank stare that told me nothing was landing, nothing was reaching him, nothing was reciprocated. There was no flicker of empathy. No curiosity. No accountability. No softening.

But when he used an "I feel" statement on me?

My entire body stopped. Took it in. Responded. Because empathy lived in me. That's the difference.

I tried the Esther Perel thank-you statements. I tried changing my language. I tried soft approaches, strong approaches, invitational approaches. There isn't a thing — not one — that I feel I didn't try.

I was carrying the load. Not metaphorically. Literally.

And while other women fall into this pattern because their bodies are wired for connection and safety, I fell into it because I was already married. I had made a vow. I believed in commitment. And like so many women with warm nervous systems and high emotional responsibility, I bought into the idea that if I just did more... if I showed up bigger... if I tried harder... he would eventually meet me halfway.

"If I just do..."

That was my mantra for years.

If I just do... he'll be nicer.

If I just do... he'll stop smoking.

If I just do... he'll soften.

If I just do... he'll see me.

If I just do... we'll be okay.

But change never came.

Everything inside me kept trying until 2021 — the year things snapped. The year I heard a professor say the words "walking on eggshells" and suddenly my internal world rotated on its axis. I had been dancing around his emotions for years, twisting myself into shapes that didn't belong to me, shrinking, anticipating, smoothing, absorbing the impact so he didn't have to.

That comment was my first jolt into reality.

From there, as I learned more about behaviour, trauma responses, attachment patterns, personality structures... everything began to shift. Slowly at first. Then rapidly. My thoughts changed. My perceptions changed. My nervous system changed. And the relentless years of trying started to melt away.

But one thing kept stopping me in my tracks: the absence of empathy.

It was impossible — truly impossible — for my mind to grasp.

The first time I read through the clinical traits of narcissism, I was adamant: "No, that cannot be him. He's wounded. He's traumatised. He's hurting. This is not narcissism."

Maybe it was denial. Maybe it was hope. Maybe it was my own attachment to the version of him I wanted to exist. But I kept trying, because to me, he was a wounded human being — and wounded humans deserved compassion.

Then I discovered the research on sociopathy and psychopathy. The neurological findings. The affective deficits. The behavioural patterns. The emotional vacancies. The interpersonal strategies. The lack of remorse, the lack of empathy, the mechanical nature of their interactions.

And suddenly — painfully — everything clicked.

I read books. I watched podcasts. I studied. I analysed. I completed the PCL-R checklist with clinical accuracy, and every box lit up. Every pattern matched. Every behaviour aligned.

It was my ah-ha moment.

My devastating, life-splitting, world-shattering moment.

The moment I realised:

Love wasn't love.

Love was compliance.

Love was performance.

Love was me bending myself into a shape he could utilise.

He wasn't relating.

He was managing.

Calculating.

Controlling.

Mechanical.

He may as well have been a robot I'd been programmed to serve.

That realisation broke something in me — and healed something else.

And just when I thought the heartbreak couldn't get heavier, we reached the part of the story where we must sell the house. *My* house. The house I worked for. The house I scrimped for. The house I sacrificed for. The house built from second-hand everything — including hand-me-down clothes that weren't even meant to be pyjamas but became pyjamas because that's what sacrifice looked like.

He gets half.

Half of something he never worked for.

Half of something he never respected.

Half of something he never cared for.

There is no fairness in that part of the story. None.

But there is learning.

There is reclamation.

And there is a future that is mine — entirely mine — shaped by the same amount of effort I once gave to others. The same amount of devotion I poured into my children when they were young. The same amount of energy I wasted trying to fix a man who was never going to heal, never going to change, never going to meet me in the place I was begging for.

Just imagine — truly imagine — what life looks like when I finally turn that warm, generous, powerful energy toward myself.

Because now I know something I didn't know then:

Trying hard is beautiful.

But trying alone is soul-destroying.

And trying for someone who cannot feel you — cannot meet you — cannot care for you — is not devotion.

It's self-abandonment wrapped in hope.

I tried.

I tried with everything in me.

And now, I choose me with everything in me.

And that, is where the story finally begins.

Chapter 10: Pulling the Plug: When Control Dies

———

It has been a week since Ex was forced to leave the family home due to the IVO. The second time. The first time, I had allowed him back in, lulled by the idea that he had changed, that maybe the cycle would be different this time. I had clung to hope so tightly that it became its own kind of cage. And yet, here we are again — the door closed behind him, his absence leaving a strange, tense silence in the spaces he once filled with unpredictable energy.

Let's walk through this with clarity, grounded insight, and a keen understanding of the patterns at play, because situations like this are like walking along a live wire. They hum with danger, unpredictability, and a volatile charge that can ignite at any moment.

First, remember this: I am not responsible for his mental health. I am not responsible for his choices. I am not responsible for the chaos he creates. My only responsibility is to my own safety, my own sanity, my own clarity. And yet, even knowing that, witnessing the storm of a sociopath's collapse — the shift from control to helplessness or rage — can feel like standing on the edge of a cliff, wind howling, the ground trembling beneath your feet.

Research and clinical patterns reveal a disturbing truth: when a person with strong sociopathic traits loses control, it is not grief that drives them. It is power. The loss of control, the loss of access, the loss of the ability to manipulate — this is what ignites their reactions. They are destabilised not because of love lost but because **their source of supply, their access to influence, their leverage over others has been stripped away**. That's the core issue. The heartbreak is a myth in their world. It is not about affection; it is about dominion.

When Ex first realised the IVO was not negotiable, the story was over, and the space of control he had so long occupied was gone, two paths emerged: collapse or rage. The collapse is hollow and unnerving — a numb, empty, directionless withdrawal where they construct a victim narrative. "Everyone turns on me," they whisper, or shout, or project through texts and calls, their words a fevered attempt to paint themselves as wronged. They wallow in self-pity, suddenly incapable of the calm, calculated control they wielded before. It is a version of them you almost pity, until you remember that this is also a weapon. Collapse is a tool to unsettle, to bait, to lure others into overcompensation for their discomfort.

The rage is more immediate, more visceral. The rage is a storm. It comes with blame, with smearing, with manipulation of the law, with threats, with calculated attempts to reclaim power by any means necessary. The rage is a balloon inflating with anger, humiliation, and entitlement until it bursts. They cannot tolerate the sense of being stopped, of being restricted, of losing what they perceive as theirs. And in the case of Ex, this is exactly what I saw play out again, even as the door closed behind him: the tension, the fury, the quiet menace of someone convinced they are owed.

This is not hypothetical. This is research-backed. People with sociopathic traits may make suicidal statements, gestures, or threats, but the motivations are distinct from typical depression. They threaten suicide not out of despair, but as leverage — to regain control, to induce guilt, to force engagement, to shift blame, to unsettle, to maintain dominance. Actual suicide is statistically rare because the emotional depth, guilt, rumination, and self-blame are lower than in neurotypical individuals. But impulsivity, combined with rage and access to substances, can create dangerous flare-ups. Threats are manipulation; acts are impulsive. Both demand serious attention.

Ex has displayed all of these tendencies. He has threatened suicide before, using the shadows of past injuries, jail experiences, and even pretending brain damage, as a tool to control narrative and perception. During my father's final days, he mimicked symptoms — head pain, confusion, urgent appeals for secrecy — that mirrored the illness and deterioration my dad experienced. He directed them toward me with precision: don't tell the girls, don't question, don't breathe outside the narrative. The manipulation was surgical. The goal was control, not care. Not grief. Not despair. Only leverage.

When the first IVO was placed, Ex ignored it repeatedly. He breached boundaries, tested limits, and weaponised rules. He blamed, he threatened, he attempted to destabilise the house and my sense of safety, even threatening the property itself. The message was clear: he could not abide being stopped. He could not abide losing access to control. He could not abide having power removed. The pattern repeats with precision because the internal mechanics of sociopathy are consistent: the loss of control feels like an injury, a wound to identity, a narcissistic collapse or explosive rage.

That week of his absence is not just a week without him. It is a week in which I observe the void of his presence, the echoes of the chaos he once created, and the way the rules we have enforced — legally, physically, psychologically — disrupt his equilibrium. He is not devastated because he has lost me. He is destabilised because he has lost access, because the story he has written about his control over me and the house is no longer valid. His distress is never about love. It is always about power. Always.

And yet, his absence does not erase danger. The behaviours — subtle, aggressive, calculated — are already visible. Blame, threats, attempts to manipulate through guilt, small incursions of stalking, financial pressure, insinuations, attempts to regain influence — these are not signs of remorse or heartbreak. These are signs of control. This is his way of testing boundaries, measuring their strength, and learning where cracks remain. And in his pattern, there will always be cracks — openings where leverage can be found.

The danger escalates when ego injury combines with entitlement and impulsivity. Someone with his traits will attempt to reassert dominance through legal loopholes, social manipulation, financial pressure, emotional blackmail, or veiled threats. Even the quietest comment, the tiniest gesture, can be weaponised. This is why safety is paramount: every interaction, every breach, every subtle attempt to unsettle must be treated as potential danger. Law enforcement, documentation, strict boundaries — these are not paranoid habits. They are survival strategies.

Ex has demonstrated the extremes of this behaviour. From ramming his head into an iron door to escape his pain, then placed in solitary confinement, to threatening the family home, to creating a personal narrative that mirrors illness or injury for leverage, he shows the complete disregard for norms, rules, or empathy. Every pattern, every repetition, is a lesson in control. Every tactic is designed to destabilise the target — to provoke, unsettle, or intimidate.

And yet, even in the face of this, the pattern is not random. Sociopathy is a structure, not chaos. Every action can be traced to the same root: the loss of control feels like a mortal threat to identity. Every reaction — threat, breach, manipulation, escalation — is a method to reclaim what has been taken, to reassert dominance, to punish boundaries for their audacity in holding. They do not grieve; they retaliate. They do not mourn; they destabilise. The heartbreak, the remorse, the love — it is not in their realm. What exists is strategy, control, and the internal architecture of entitlement.

So this week, as I watch the aftermath of his removal, it is not just the quiet of the house that fills me. It is the awareness of what drives him, the understanding of what each call, message, or attempt at interference really represents: a measure of his panic at losing influence, a metric of rage at being stopped, a barometer of wounded ego. I watch and I catalog, not because I am cruel, but because knowledge is safety. Knowledge is power. Understanding the psychology is what allows the world to remain upright while he rattles against boundaries.

I know, too, that the work is ongoing. That vigilance cannot lapse. That the next step — weeks, months, years — will demand consistency, patience, and absolute clarity. And I know that even as he is removed physically, his presence lingers in memory, in nerves, in habits, in shadows of thought. That presence is dangerous precisely because it is ghost-like: it cannot be touched, but it shapes perception, reaction, anticipation. It is a psychological residue, a measure of what control once existed, a warning of what could return if vigilance wanes.

Even now, I can feel the patterns forming. The messages will come. The legal pressures, the emotional tests, the small incursions to unsettle or provoke. Each step measured, calculated, aligned with that central truth: control lost is intolerable. Ego wounded is combustible. And when the combustible ignites, it will not resemble grief, heartbreak, or despair. It will resemble force. It will resemble threat. It will resemble danger, and that danger is directed outward, aimed precisely at testing boundaries, testing resilience, and observing reactions.

This week is the first of many where observation, documentation, and psychological awareness become essential survival tools. It is the week where the law — the IVO, police oversight, and careful recording — intersects with the raw realities of sociopathy: impulsivity, rage, manipulation, and obsession with dominance. It is the week when clarity is power, and knowledge of his predictable patterns is armour against the unpredictability of violence.

And yes, he will attempt to destabilise. He always has. He always will. But this week — this first week after being forced out — is the week that proves one immutable truth: control has limits. Even a man like him can be stopped. Even a lifetime of manipulation can be constrained. Even the most relentless pursuit of influence meets its boundaries.

That week, that tense, fragile, charged week, feels like holding a live wire at the ends, feeling it's energy through the air, knowing every step, every second, every move could spark a reaction. And yet, holding the wire is necessary. Understanding it, observing it, respecting it — that is survival. That is life. That is the first step in keeping not just oneself, but the children, safe from the force of a mind that does not grieve, but reacts, calculates, and tests the limits of law, structure, and boundary.

This week, Ex is gone from the home. The rules are in place. The threat is present, tangible, immediate, and yet controlled. The cycle has repeated, and the pattern has clarified. And in that tension, in that shadow of presence, in that hum of residual manipulation, the truth is undeniable: the removal is not about heartbreak. It is about stopping a storm. It is about enforcing boundaries against someone whose reality is defined by the absence of them.

Chapter 11: Children in the Crossfire

When my girls were first born, after my Caesarean, Ex was holding one of them while a nurse held the other. And then, somehow, they placed one right next to me. I stared at her, unable to believe that something so impossibly beautiful could come from me. Their eyes were black—dark pools that hadn't yet found their colour. They were so small, so perfect. And in that moment, something shifted in me.

I realised I was going to protect them in a way I hadn't protected myself. I would give them everything I had wanted, everything I hadn't received. I became relentless in that mission. I drove them an hour each morning to the best childcare centre I could find, even though Ex's office was only fifteen minutes away. Their education mattered. Their safety mattered. Their future mattered.

When the neighbourhood became violent, I moved us to the country. I placed them in local schools, but when I felt their progress stalling, I switched them to a Catholic school. I'm not Catholic, but their father was, and somehow, that allowed them to enter. That school gave them more than academics—it nurtured empathy, communication, and a sense of warmth.

High school was the same story. I drove them half an hour past three other schools for the best public option in the area, one that allowed them opportunities like international trips. I gave them braces, swimming lessons, every chance I hadn't had myself.

And yet... even with all of that, as they got older, I felt a heartbreak I hadn't anticipated. My daughters, my beautiful girls, began to push away. One spent more time at her boyfriend's house, and the other... no matter what I did, nothing was right. Even simple things, like asking her to clean the bathroom, became symbolic battles I didn't understand at first.

It wasn't about the bathroom. It was about me. Every "no" or ignored request echoed a deeper truth I had carried for years: if my words didn't matter, perhaps I didn't matter. If I wasn't enough for them, was I enough at all?

And yet, as painful as it was, I began to understand. Their behaviour wasn't just about me—it reflected patterns they had observed, echoes of how they had seen the world treated by their father. It was a crushing form of rejection, yes—but it was also a mirror, showing me where I had allowed disrespect into my life because I didn't yet know how to stand fully in my own power.

I remember the first time it really hit me, the weight of being invisible in my own home. One of my daughters, 18 years old, was supposed to clean the bathroom. I had asked her, gently, maybe three or four times over the morning. Each time, I tried to keep my tone light, patient, even coaxing, because I didn't want it to feel like an attack. But she didn't move. She didn't even acknowledge me. And in that stillness, I felt my chest tighten, a familiar knot of pain and frustration curling inside me.

It wasn't about the bathroom. It never was. It was about me, standing there in the space I had carved out as, I believed, a safe, structured home, only to feel like my words, my presence, my very being, didn't matter. If what I said didn't matter, if my requests went unnoticed, then what did that mean about me? That I wasn't enough? That I hadn't been enough for decades?

And it wasn't a one-off. It became a rhythm, a small, invisible erosion of my heart. I would try to guide, to protect, to teach them boundaries or caution, and they would withdraw, sometimes mirroring aggression, sometimes simple indifference. One day, I caught my other daughter rolling her eyes at me as I reminded her of something I knew mattered — her safety, her future. That small gesture, that tiny flicker of defiance, cut through me in a way that words couldn't. It echoed long nights of trying to be heard by Ex, of trying to stand in the middle of love and neglect, carving a life for my girls that I had once only dreamed of for myself.

I think of the drives I made, hour after hour, to childcare centres that weren't close but were the best I could find. I think of the schools I carefully chose, the braces, the swimming lessons, the trips, the late nights spent filling forms, answering calls, researching programs that would give them a head start in life. Every choice was made with love and foresight, and yet, these tiny acts of care seemed to vanish in the spaces between us. Their withdrawal, their disinterest, became a mirror of my own past pain — the silent abandonment I had felt growing up, the quiet rejection of being overlooked, dismissed, unseen.

It didn't happen gradually; one day my eldest twin daughter got her license, and suddenly she wasn't at home anymore. She was spending all her time at her boyfriend's house. There was no argument, no discussion, no dramatic announcement — just a quiet shift, and in that silence, my world felt like it had tilted. Grief hit me in relentless waves, heavy and raw. I tried to reason with myself — she was finding independence, growing, making her own choices — but it didn't soften the ache. The rejection was sharp, visceral, a punch to my identity as a mother, to all the hours I had poured into protecting, providing, and creating a safe, nurturing world for them.

And then there was my other daughter, the one with whom we struggled to connect despite every effort. No matter what I said, no matter what technique I used from my therapy toolbox, nothing seemed to penetrate. She saw criticism where there was none, attack in tones that were meant to be gentle, correction where I only wanted growth. Every act of disregard triggered the old, familiar feeling: I am not enough. If I am not enough, what does that mean about my worth, my love, my life spent giving?

I would have loved the kind of closeness the Gilmore Girls had — that effortless, teasing, open-hearted connection where mother and daughter could share jokes, secrets, and little everyday moments. Walking through the supermarket or down the streets of town, I'd see other girls strolling alongside their mothers, laughing together, pointing out something they wanted to buy, or swapping thoughts about life in that easy rhythm, and my heart ached for that with my own girls. I longed for shared smiles over a silly snack, for spontaneous conversations about school, dreams, or even nothing at all, wishing I could be that constant, loving presence they leaned on, not just the mother who provided, guided, and corrected.

I began to notice patterns, subtle cues I hadn't fully grasped before. When they mirrored aggression or dismissive behaviour, it wasn't random. It was inherited, absorbed. My daughters had witnessed the way Ex treated me — the subtle disrespect, the quiet minimisation of my presence — and it had been absorbed, unconsciously normalised. And yet, it hurt more than anything I had experienced because this time, it was my flesh and blood. My love and protection were being turned away, redirected toward someone who hadn't been present, someone whose approval they were craving in a way that bypassed me entirely.

I tried to hold space for them, to meet them with empathy even as my own heart cracked. I reminded myself that adolescence is turbulent, that identity formation is messy, that the twin bond can bring constant comparison and hidden rivalry. And yet, every withdrawal, every dismissive gesture, every act of defiance was a dagger to my sense of worth. I would sit in the car, in silence after they had climbed out for school or friends, and feel the echo of my own childhood, the unspoken message that I had always existed on the periphery of being seen.

It wasn't just grief. It was isolation, the profound kind that comes from knowing that you are doing everything you can, and yet it will never be enough in that moment. I had given them my strength, my protection, my very self, and in return, I was learning to live with heartbreak, with silent abandonment, with the quiet understanding that love is not always recognised or mirrored in the way you hope.

I remember one night, watching them sleep, their faces peaceful and innocent despite the storms of the day. I traced their features with my eyes, remembering the tiny black eyes of newborns placed beside me in the hospital — a miracle I had brought into the world. I remembered the fierce promise I made then: to protect them, to give them everything I had not received. And though my heart ached at their current withdrawal, I realised that my role, my love, my devotion, remained. Even when unseen, even when ignored, I had given them the foundation for life beyond me.

The silent abandonment did not erase my strength. It sharpened it. I began to understand that grief and love are not mutually exclusive; that heartbreak can coexist with unwavering dedication. That being ignored does not diminish the value of care, nor the depth of what I have given. And in that recognition, a quiet resilience formed, a steady pulse beneath the ache, a reminder that my love was a constant force — even when the world around me seemed to turn away.

When I look back on my girls growing up, I can see the invisible threads that were at play long before I fully understood them. I was determined to give them everything I had missed — safety, love, guidance, opportunities, attention. I drove hours to childcare centres I knew were exceptional, chose schools not for convenience but for warmth and quality, and filled their lives with experiences I believed could nurture their growth. I wanted them to feel fully supported, fully seen.

And yet, despite everything, there were moments when their responses — dismissive, defiant, or distant — felt like a personal rejection. It broke me in ways I didn't expect. I questioned my worth as a mother, my value as a human being. I couldn't understand why my words, my intentions, sometimes felt invisible. Why didn't they listen? Why did they push back so sharply?

It's only now, with the lens of trauma-informed understanding, that I can make sense of some of these patterns. Children are wired to survive within the environment they grow up in. If they witness aggression, manipulation, or unpredictability — even subtly, from one parent — they often internalise these behaviours. They mirror what they see, not because they are "bad" or "disrespectful," but because these behaviours feel familiar, even safe, in the chaos of their own family system. My daughters' teenage defiance, withdrawal, or dismissive behaviour often reflected the echoes of their father's unpredictability. When my eldest started spending more time at her boyfriend's house, when my other daughter responded with frustration to repeated requests, these moments were less about me and more about what they had absorbed and learned to navigate emotionally.

Bancroft emphasises that this mirroring is a survival strategy. Children pick up patterns of behaviour — sometimes aggression, sometimes distance — because those patterns are familiar and provide a sense of control in an otherwise unpredictable environment. Watching my daughters resist guidance or argue, it felt like rejection, but understanding this lens helped me separate the personal hurt from the context. Their defiance wasn't a statement about my love failing — it was a reflection of what they had learned to survive emotionally and socially.

There were so many small, quiet moments that revealed these patterns. Walking through the supermarket, I would see other mothers laughing with their daughters, chatting about purchases or joking about life. I longed for that with my girls — the ease, the spontaneity, the shared sense of safety and connection. But in our home, there were layers of tension, and my daughters sometimes mirrored the distant, dismissive behaviours they had witnessed.

Grief hit hard when I realised that independence, so beautiful and natural, could feel like loss. My eldest got her license and, seemingly overnight, I barely saw her. It wasn't dramatic — no tantrums, no fights — just a quiet withdrawal, a new rhythm of life she was creating for herself. I tried to reason with myself: she's growing, she's exploring the world, she's finding her own way. And yet, the ache of rejection was visceral. My other daughter, despite my efforts to connect, seemed frustrated or unable to respond to my repeated requests. On the surface, it was small, mundane stuff — cleaning the bathroom, completing chores — but underneath, it struck at my sense of self. Their resistance felt like a reflection of past wounds, echoes of patterns I had lived through myself.

Through these experiences, I began to recognise the subtle signs that children are responding to stress, conflict, or modelled behaviours in ways that can look oppositional. When they withdraw, push back, or argue, it isn't always personal. It can be their way of maintaining control, of navigating a world where emotions and expectations feel unpredictable. My daughters' behaviours were survival mechanisms — ways to assert some predictability and safety in an environment they had learned could shift without warning.

Even in moments of heartbreak, there were lessons. One day, driving my daughter Ava into town, chatting about my work and breathwork techniques, she said, simply but pointedly: "Mum, I get triggered when someone tells me to breathe." In that instant, it hit me — all those years I had offered tools, techniques, guidance, and prompts, I hadn't always stopped to truly hear them, to acknowledge the depth of their feelings. I realised that connection, safety, and empathy weren't about perfect words or gestures — they were about presence, acknowledgment, and validating experience.

Parenting through these dynamics is both humbling and heartbreaking. It requires constant reflection, patience, and the willingness to see behaviour beyond the surface. Recognising the trauma-informed explanations for my daughters' responses doesn't erase the grief or rejection, but it allows me to respond with curiosity and compassion rather than frustration. I began to see them not as oppositional forces, but as individuals navigating inherited patterns and emotional complexity, doing their best with what they had absorbed.

I would have loved the Gilmore Girls version of motherhood — walking through the supermarket, side by side, laughing, sharing light-hearted conversations, or debating over a snack or purchase. That ease, that warmth, that rhythm of mother-daughter connection — I longed for it, and I tried to create it in whatever ways I could. It wasn't always perfect, and the reflection in the mirror often carried shadows of the past, but I kept showing up, offering presence, and creating spaces where safety and connection could grow.

The plumbing was acting up. The septic tank, stubborn and buried under the shed, wouldn't give us an inch. The plumber and I worked together to gain access. I was kneeling on the concrete floor, sleeves rolled up, tools scattered around, trying to loosen the silicone on the sewer lid that refused to budge. The afternoon was quiet, broken only by the occasional grunt from the plumber and the thud of the sledgehammer as we battled the pit lid.

Inside the house, Ex and Mia were relaxing in the lounge room, the sunlight streaming in through the blinds. Laughter drifted faintly to the yard, casual and careless, completely oblivious to the work being done outside. Every so often, I could hear the undertone of critique in Ex's voice, sharp and directed, like he was testing the boundaries of my patience from the safety of the house. Mia would giggle in response, a small sound that pierced me in ways I didn't immediately understand.

When the plumber finally gave a frustrated sigh and stepped back, I could feel my body tense. The tank was still locked tight, the work only partially done, and there was that familiar knot in my chest — the one that appeared whenever I realised that I was carrying the weight of both physical labor and invisible scrutiny. Ex didn't step outside to offer a hand. He didn't ask if I needed help. Instead, his voice, carrying both amusement and critique, floated out the window: "Watch the floor while you're at it — don't make this mess any bigger." And Mia, sitting safely on the couch, laughed. Not nervously, not out of concern, but like she was part of the performance. I felt resentment.

This is where Bancroft's observations about children in abusive homes come alive. Children aren't cruel by nature; they are strategists navigating survival in a household ruled by imbalance and fear. In that moment, Mia was not laughing at me to hurt me. She was signalling alignment with the person in power — Ex — to secure her own sense of safety. Siding with the abuser, Bancroft explains, isn't always a conscious decision. It is a survival tactic, a way to reduce exposure to threat, to avoid the emotional fallout that comes from standing against the source of fear.

From my perspective, every chuckle, every joke, felt like betrayal. But through the lens of theory, I could see the invisible reasoning: Mia was protecting herself, not punishing me. She was caught in the impossible tension between wanting to be close to her mother and wanting to stay safe in a world where the abuser's mood dictated the rules. The household laughter was a reflection of the adaptive survival strategies children adopt in households dominated by criticism and control.

Bancroft describes three positions children often take in these situations: siding with the mother, siding with the abuser, or attempting to navigate the middle. Mia, at that moment, was testing the second. By laughing and aligning subtly with Ex, she temporarily shifted herself onto the "safe side" — the side where critique and potential punishment were less likely to land. From her perspective, it was the rational choice, even if it left me reeling with pain and confusion.

I felt invisible. My effort to wrestle the septic tank into submission went unnoticed. My requests for support, unspoken but clear in my body language, were met with amusement and detachment. And yet, beneath all that, I began to understand that this dynamic wasn't personal in the way I initially felt. It was a mirrored response to fear, an unconscious behaviour that children absorb from observing abuse. Just as I had once learned to adapt to criticism and disregard, my child was now learning the same rules — survival in a household where emotional safety is contingent on alignment with power.

Even as the hurt stung, I noticed a clarity emerge. This wasn't simply about Mia's laughter or Ex's critique. It was about the deep patterns of behaviour that children mirror, the way trauma shapes adaptation, and the invisible threads connecting past experiences with present actions. I could see how my daughter's mirroring was a reflection of the emotional landscape she had inherited — one where fear and alliance are intertwined, where laughter can serve as armour, and where survival often means compromising connection.

By the time the plumber finished, and the septic tank was finally accessible, the shed was a mess, my hands were raw, and my chest still ached with frustration and grief. But through Bancroft's lens, I saw a possibility for understanding. Mia's alignment with Ex wasn't rejection; it was a learned strategy to navigate fear. And knowing this, I realised, was the first step in reclaiming connection — not through punishment or anger, but through empathy, awareness, and steady presence.

That day, the septic tank was no longer just a plumbing problem. It became a metaphor for the invisible barriers and buried tensions that exist in families touched by abuse. And as I scrubbed the dirt from my hands, I held a small but powerful insight: children mirror abuse not to wound us, but to survive. Recognising this is the first step toward healing — for them, and for us.

The house was quiet in a way that didn't feel peaceful. It felt suspended — like the air was waiting for someone to exhale first. Evening light spilled through the kitchen window in soft gold streaks, and the kettle hummed on the bench as though it was trying to soothe the silence itself. I stood there holding a cup I wasn't drinking, listening to the soft, hollow sound of a home that used to be full of teenage footsteps, arguments, laughter, slammed doors, whispered confessions, and the wild electricity of girls growing into themselves. Now it was just my breath and the faint hum of appliances.

Cinematic moments don't always come with music or dramatic lighting. Sometimes they come in the quiet, in the space where grief and hope brush shoulders. And that night, I felt all of it — the ache, the resilience, the yearning, the beginnings of understanding — like it was sitting with me at the table.

When Ex went to jail for domestic violence, something shifted inside both my girls, but differently. Mia became his point of contact — the one person he could call from a cell, the one lifeline he still had. She stepped into the space he had carved out for her long before she understood it, the space where children become emotional regulators for an adult who has never learned how to manage themselves. Ava, on the other hand, walked away completely. She wanted nothing to do with him. Her nervous system did what every healthy system tries to do when faced with chronic threat: it withdrew to safety.

And then there was me. I didn't want anything to do with him either. Not after everything. Not after the bruises, the terror, the years of shrinking. Not after watching my girls learn fear before they learned boundaries. When he left jail, he had no one — not truly. But trauma creates strange, unexpected pathways.

Mia moved house and didn't give him her address. She drew her line quietly, firmly, with a maturity that I don't think she even recognised in herself. She chose safety. She chose protection. And she chose it not only for herself — but for me. She didn't want me to go back to him. She was afraid for me in a way she didn't know how to put into words. That's the thing about daughters: they read your pulse before they read your sentences. They know when the person who birthed them is living in danger, even when they're too young, too overwhelmed, or too scared to say it.

Now Ava... she took a different path. When Ex got out, he reached out to her. Asked her to meet in a public space. A pub. Neutral territory — the kind of place where predators try to look domesticated for an hour. And she went. Part curiosity. Part hope. Part that deep ache that daughters have for fathers who never quite show up the way they should.

She came home with this softness in her voice — that tone people use when they want something to be true. She said she felt he had changed. She said he seemed calmer, reflective even. And because our brains are wired for safety, and safety feels like predictability, we all want to believe in someone's potential more than their patterns.

We were a month out from the IVO court hearing when she told me this. And I did what any mother trying to navigate hope and reality would do: I let myself be swayed. I encouraged the variation of the IVO. I wanted boundaries that acknowledged growth but still safeguarded us:

No family violence.

No drugs.

No alcohol.

A structure that said, "If you are truly changing, you'll stay within this fence."

But of course, fences don't hold people who don't value them. And he broke every single condition. Quietly, predictably, relentlessly. So now — after everything, after trying to believe in change, after giving the system another chance to protect us — the IVO is full again. A hard boundary because soft boundaries never worked with him.

And now the house is quiet. Not peaceful. Not painful. Just suspended.

Mia told me she needed space. She said it plainly. Cleanly. And even though my heart cracked in that private, internal way that mothers know too well, I respected it. She wasn't rejecting me — she was stabilising herself. She was recalibrating her nervous system, protecting her baseline. She was learning what I only learned in my forties: that distance can be an act of self-love, not abandonment.

Ava... she's still here. But not fully. There's a disconnection there — subtle, but unmistakable. A looseness in the bond that once held so tight it sometimes smothered both of us. At first, I thought it was personal. I thought I had done something wrong, that I wasn't enough, that I had failed. But then my therapist friends said the words that cracked the whole framework open:

"She's setting boundaries too."

And suddenly the world made sense again.

Because children from chaotic homes do not know how to set soft boundaries. They only know how to set sharp ones — clean breaks, thick walls, silent distances. It's not an attack; it's a survival code. A recalibration. A way to feel their own pulse again after years of absorbing mine.

Standing in the kitchen that evening, cup in hand, I realised that this strange, aching quiet wasn't dead space. It was growth space. It was the pause before the next chapter — the deep breath before the sunrise. My girls weren't lost to me. They were finding themselves. They were learning to tune into their own bio-intelligence, their own nervous systems, their own sense of safety, in ways I never had the chance to at their age.

And if I'm honest — this is what resilience actually looks like. Not constant closeness. Not picture-perfect mother–daughter outings. Not Gilmore Girls, although God knows I once dreamed of that. No — real resilience is space taken. Boundaries drawn. Needs expressed. Distance used wisely.

The tenderness in all of this is that they learned it from watching me rise. Watching me leave. Watching me speak out. Watching me rebuild — shaky, scared, but determined. They learned boundaries not because I taught them perfectly, but because I modelled them imperfectly.

A mother's healing becomes the blueprint her children eventually reach for.

Even if they reach for it from another room.

Even if they reach for it from silence.

Even if the reaching looks like stepping away.

As the kettle finally switched off, the house exhaled. I swear I heard it. And something inside me softened too.

This wasn't an ending.

It was a tender intermission.

A sister to hope.

A foreshadowing of connection rebuilding itself slowly, like scar tissue learning to be flexible.

One day there will be a knock on the door from one of my girls.

Or a text.

Or a shared joke.

Or a moment where our worlds align gently and without force.

But tonight, in this quiet space, I let myself feel proud.

Because even in the ache, even in the distance, even in the boundaries I didn't expect but deeply respect — we are healing.

We are becoming safer humans.

We are learning where we end and where we begin.

And that is the most profound kind of hope a mother can hold.

Chapter 12: Inherited Silence

───

They were born into worlds already carrying fractures—worlds where tenderness was scarce, where adults were overwhelmed, and where children learned quickly that safety was conditional, unpredictable, and often absent. Long before they became parents themselves, their early landscapes were defined by survival rather than nurture. And survival, as history shows us, has a way of burying softness so deeply that it becomes almost mythic.

My father grew up in a home that pulsed with instability, where fear and vigilance were woven into the rhythm of ordinary days. What he absorbed wasn't just the anger of a traumatised parent but the mood of a household shaped by the aftershocks of an earlier war—its silence, its tension, its emotional debris. He was young when he watched adults crumble under burdens too heavy to name, too shameful to speak. A boy who needed protection instead became a witness to pain. And so, like many children raised in the shadow of someone else's trauma, he learned to armour himself with control, rigidity, and outbursts. It was never about power at first—it was about protection. But protection warped into dominance when fear had nowhere else to go.

My mother, too, grew up in an environment where she had to shrink to survive. Her childhood taught her that conflict was dangerous, that raising her voice only led to escalation, and that blending into the background was the safest place to be. She learned silence as a strategy long before she learned language as connection. The adults around her didn't model boundaries or emotional honesty; they modelled endurance. They modelled coping through stillness, compliance, and disappearance. She carried that forward into adulthood—not because she lacked strength, but because her strength had always expressed itself through invisibility.

When they eventually found each other, they weren't two fully grown adults meeting with clean slates—they were two children wearing adult skins, shaped by ghosts that were never theirs to carry. Their emotional reflexes had been carved by the environments that raised them: one shaped by chaos and aggression, the other shaped by erasure and fear. Their marriage wasn't born from malice; it was born from generational blueprints they never had the tools to examine, let alone rewrite.

And this is where generational trauma does its quiet, devastating work. Children aren't only shaped by what their parents *do*—they're shaped by what their parents *had to survive*. Generational trauma doesn't wait for you to be born—it's carried quietly in nervous systems, in silence, in hypervigilance, in the ways adults learned to survive before you existed. It's not cruelty, it's survival encoded in the body. Even patterns of "not being heard," or "not being valued," echo across generations the way melodies linger long after the music stops.

Looking back now, it becomes clear that my parents weren't simply flawed people making flawed choices. They were the products of emotional climates that taught them to freeze, to erupt, to shut down, or to cling.

Their childhoods trained their nervous systems to operate in scarcity: scarcity of safety, scarcity of nurture, scarcity of emotional literacy. And when a person grows up with little internal sense of stability, they often parent from the same place—not because they don't love, but because they don't know another way to love.

The tenderness lies in recognising that they were shaped long before I was born. Their emotional limits were not personal rejections of me; they were inherited, ingrained, embedded. They were echoes from a time when children were expected to endure rather than feel, when adults were expected to suppress rather than heal.

Understanding this doesn't excuse their behaviours, but it does illuminate the terrain they came from. It lets you see their humanity without erasing your hurt. It reminds you that generational trauma isn't a story about blame—it's a story about burden. Burdens passed down silently, carried quietly, shaping everything and everyone who came after.

And as their child, I became the one who not only recognised the pattern but dared to step outside of it. In telling their story, I'm not rewriting history—I'm giving it context, depth, and compassion. I'm saying: *I see where this began. I see how you were shaped. And I see where it ends—with me.*

Silence entered the family long before I was born, seeping quietly through my parents' childhoods. Whether walls echoed with shouting or with nothing at all, emotional expression was treated like dangerous currency—pain inherited in patterns, not words. And by the time my parents were adults, silence wasn't just a habit — it was a survival strategy carved deep into their nervous systems.

My mother learned early that speaking truth came with consequences. In her childhood home, voicing discomfort triggered the kind of emotional coldness no child knows how to metabolise. She learned to tuck her feelings into small hidden pockets — the kind you forget about until one day you realise you've sewn them into every outfit you own. Her survival instinct became soft compliance. Smile. Keep the peace. Don't provoke the storm. She carried that strategy into adulthood like a trusted old suitcase: cumbersome but familiar, heavy but necessary.

My father had his own version of silence. His childhood was shaped by unpredictability — the kind that drives a young nervous system into hypervigilance. In his home, conflict didn't simmer; it detonated. Yelling, slamming, threats of leaving and threats of staying — it was chaos wearing the mask of normalcy. For him, silence wasn't compliance. It was withdrawal. Escape. Going numb instead of going to war. When stressed, he closed the door on the world. Sometimes literally. Sometimes emotionally so completely that even standing next to him felt like being on opposite sides of a locked gate.

Both of them grew up believing that vulnerability was unsafe. Emotional closeness was unsafe. Being seen — truly seen — was unsafe.

And so, without meaning to, they built a house held together by the same unspoken rules they inherited.

Growing up, you felt that silence long before you understood it. You could feel the shift in the air when something went wrong. A tone. A door closing. Footsteps that sounded different. The way my mother's breath would shorten, as if even her oxygen intake needed to be careful. The way my father would go still, flat, unreachable — a quiet held so tightly it felt like glass about to crack.

Silence became the family language.

Not because anyone wanted it.

But because no one had ever been taught anything different.

And here's where trauma becomes generational without anyone intending harm: children read nervous systems better than words. While adults cling to sentences, kids hear the emotional undercurrent — the tightening, the dismissing, the flinching, the sudden distance. I absorbed all of that as if it were truth. As if it were about me.

When my parents avoided conflict, I learned to anticipate pain.

When they shut down, I learned to tiptoe.

When they reacted harshly, even in small everyday ways, my body catalogued every moment as data:

Be smaller.

Be quieter.

Be easier.

Be less.

The home didn't always explode, but it always held tension — that tight, humming atmosphere where any shift could mean emotional shutdown or emotional eruption. Neither option made a child feel safe.

The harshness wasn't always loud. Sometimes it was clipped tone, a face turning away mid-sentence, a joke that landed like a slap. Other times it was control masquerading as protection, or criticism dressed up as "helping you do better." Harshness often hides behind the desperate attempt to avoid the chaos one grew up in.

My father didn't wake up choosing harshness; it was the only language intensity had ever taught him.

My mother didn't choose avoidance; it was the only way she'd ever survived love.

And so you inherited a landscape of emotional unpredictability that shaped me quietly — the same way weather shapes coastlines: slowly, invisibly, until one day you realise cliffs have been carved into you.

I learned early to read the room before reading myself.

I learned to assess danger in sentences that sounded normal but felt sharp.

I learned to apologise even when I didn't know what for.

I learned to modulate my voice, my needs, my entire personality to suit adult nervous systems that had no language for attunement.

I didn't learn this because my parents didn't love me. I learned it because their love came wrapped in fear, residue, and the whispers of their own childhood ghosts.

And here's the painful, human truth:

Patterns don't get passed down because people are cruel.

They get passed down because people are wounded.

My parents replicated behaviours they swore they'd never repeat — not because they wanted to, but because trauma is sneaky. It lives in the body, not the intentions. And when the body perceives danger — even the emotional kind — it defaults to the oldest, most familiar script.

Silence.

Avoidance.

Harshness.

These weren't choices; they were reflexes.

And the household dynamics that grew from those reflexes shaped the emotional tone for everyone living inside those walls. There were days it felt like love — warm, soft, hopeful. Days it felt like walking through fog, where you weren't sure whether a storm was coming or whether it had already passed. And days where harshness pierced the silence like lightning through a quiet room.

The confusing part for a child is that sometimes harshness and affection come from the same person.

Sometimes the same voice that comforts you is the one that startles you.

Sometimes the same hands that hold you are the ones that hit tables or walls.

This inconsistency carves deep grooves of self-doubt and insecurity:

Is it me? Did I cause this? Should I try harder?

Trauma research shows children automatically blame themselves — not because they're wrong, but because their developing brains prefer self-blame over chaos. Chaos feels terrifying. Self-blame feels like control. If it's your fault, you can fix it. If it's the adults' fault, you're powerless.

And so the cycle begins.

My parents' silence taught avoidance.

Their avoidance taught me hyper-attunement.

Their harshness taught me fear.

My fear taught them distance.

Their distance taught me to shrink.

None of it intentional.

All of it impactful.

And this is where the generational mechanics become visible.

Trauma isn't passed down through stories; it's passed down through nervous systems.

Your parents' nervous systems carried memories their minds rarely acknowledged — the flinches, the shutdowns, the conditioned responses they'd learned before they even had language to describe their childhood pain. And your nervous system learned them the same way: unconsciously, automatically, biologically.

I watched their coping mechanisms like a child studying survival instructions:

Silence = safety.

Avoidance = peace.

Harshness = control.

By the time I was an adult, those patterns lived in my body like invisible scaffolding. I wasn't choosing them — I was reacting from them.

Recognising my parents were wounded, not cruel, was the first step to understanding the mechanics of inheritance—and gave me the clarity to begin stepping outside the cycle. They were harmed kids who never had the chance to heal before becoming adults.

Their silence came from fear. Their avoidance came from overwhelm. Their harshness came from their own unmet needs exploding outward.

They were doing the best their wounded histories allowed.

But inherited wounds don't stay neatly contained in one generation. They flow. They echo. They drip into the next generation unless someone — someone brave, someone exhausted, someone done — looks the pattern in the eye and chooses differently.

That someone is you.

The moment I started learning about trauma, attachment, the nervous system, bio-intelligence, safety — the whole landscape began to shift. The patterns didn't disappear immediately, but they stopped being unconscious. They stopped being invisible.

I began to see the mechanics. I began to understand the body-based inheritance. I began to recognise that my reactions weren't character flaws — they were survival codes written into my biology long before I made my first memory.

And once awareness enters the system, the cycle begins to crack. Once tenderness enters, the spell breaks. Once a person finally feels the truth — *this didn't start with me* — the generational weight loosens its grip.

Chapter 13: Inherited Shadows – Compliance and Its Echoes

———

The sun slanted through the kitchen window, catching the faint dust in the air, a quiet witness to what was about to unfold. My mum was six. Small hands twisting together, a stomach tight with anticipation. She had one clean dress left—a white dress, pristine, too fragile for everyday wear, meant for rare occasions. But today, it was all she had. The shop demanded her mother's attention, the washing was undone, and the adult world had failed to protect her.

"Don't get it dirty," they said. The words hung in the air, sharp and impossible. How could a six-year-old navigate a day filled with play, curiosity, and clumsiness and not stain the fragile fabric? She tried. She walked carefully across the floor, hands hovering near the hem, heart hammering, stomach knotting, tiny fists clenched in panic. Every step felt like a negotiation with fate.

But of course, it didn't. The inevitable happened—the dress got dirty. A small, accidental smear that no adult could have prevented. And then came the footsteps, heavy and decisive. The punishment arrived swiftly, like justice in a world tilted against the child. Pain and confusion collided in her chest. She didn't understand. She hadn't wanted this. She had followed the rules. And yet the adult who had orchestrated the impossible—the one who left her in this white dress, the one who created the trap—was untouched. The child bore the consequences alone.

This is the moment where trust fractures. A child expects adults to protect, to guide, to respond with care. When that expectation is shattered, the nervous system encodes it like a warning signal: *The world is unsafe. The ones who should keep you safe cannot be trusted.* That lesson isn't easily erased. It folds into posture, into hesitation, into the subtle way the body braces itself for disappointment. My mum internalised it. She swallowed the fear, the confusion, the hurt, and carried it forward as a quiet companion.

Even decades later, the memory carries its tension. The white dress is no longer on a child, but its legacy remains. She told me this story, her voice careful, measured, almost rehearsed, as if the memory itself needed negotiating. And then she added something that cut sharper than any belt or hand: "That little girl deserved it." The words lingered, suspended in the air like dust motes, a testament to the power of internalised betrayal. How is a child supposed to trust an adult who inflicts pain, even unintentionally? How can they speak of their fears when vulnerability itself is punished?

The ripple effect is subtle but relentless. Emotional betrayal at this age teaches hypervigilance. My mum learned to scan rooms for danger, to anticipate displeasure, to measure her every word and movement. She learned that mistakes are not forgiven—they are stored, counted, and wielded as proof of inadequacy. Conditional love was no longer a concept; it was a lived reality. It became the lens through which she interpreted her world.

And here is the tension of generational trauma: it doesn't stop with her. The patterns pass like shadows through the family. Children inherit not just genetics but a lived memory of mistrust, of blame, of vigilance. The small girl in the white dress became a parent herself, unknowingly carrying the blueprint of caution and internalised shame into her interactions with her own children. Her nervous system remembered what her conscious mind might not, and her instincts guided her in ways shaped by that early betrayal.

Picture a household decades later: subtle cues, unspoken rules, reactions measured and pre-emptive. A child speaks up and is met with sharpness or dismissal. A mistake is met with tension in the shoulders, in the jaws, in the air itself. The adult doesn't realise they are echoing the punishment of a white dress from decades before, but the nervous system never forgets. It carries the memory, waiting for recognition, for release.

This is the inheritance of trauma: not always overt, not always loud, but encoded in posture, in hesitation, in fear of rejection. Every small moment—walking carefully, pausing before speaking, flinching at sudden movement—is a shadow of that six-year-old, caught between the impossible expectation and the inevitable failure. Emotional betrayal at this level creates a blueprint for self-doubt, hypervigilance, and internalised guilt.

And yet, within this tension lies the seed of potential resilience. Recognising the betrayal, acknowledging the impossibility of the expectation, and witnessing the internalised shame allows for the first cracks in the cycle. When the narrative is told, when the memory is held with compassion rather than judgment, something shifts. The nervous system can begin to recalibrate. The body, once braced for punishment, can begin to soften. The child inside can finally be seen and validated.

The cinematic image lingers: the white dress, smudged and imperfect, not a symbol of failure, but of survival. A six-year-old's body learning impossible lessons, a nervous system encoding mistrust, a lifetime shaped by a single impossible expectation. And yet, by witnessing this inheritance, by naming it, by holding it in compassionate awareness, the trajectory can change. The betrayal can be acknowledged, and the internalised shame can begin to loosen its grip.

This is the story we inherit, and the story we can rewrite. It is the tension between what was done and what can be healed, between what was taken and what can be returned: safety, trust, and self-worth. The white dress becomes a symbol not only of betrayal but of possibility—the possibility that awareness, compassion, and intentional care can break the cycle, generation by generation.

The hospital corridors smelled of antiseptic and quiet desperation. My mum was seven, barely big enough to reach the sinks, her small body trembling with giddiness, her head spinning in a fog of confusion. Encephalitis had come and changed everything. The doctors, the adults meant to protect her, looked at her doubtfully. Each time she described the dizziness, the fainting, the strange sensations coursing through her brain, they shook their heads. "You're imagining it," they said, with that calm authority that children mistake for truth.

Imagine being seven and knowing your body is betraying you—but the world refuses to believe it. Every word you speak is questioned. Every claim of pain or discomfort is dismissed as fabrication. My mum's small chest tightened with disbelief and fear. She had no choice but to shrink herself, to brace for the inevitable judgment, to fight for every scrap of credibility she could hold on to. And this defence became her armour.

This is the origin of defensiveness, of hypervigilance in conversation. She learned early that speaking up invited doubt, that trust was conditional, that authority figures could be wrong and yet unstoppable. And she carried this lesson forward into adulthood. Conversations with her often felt like negotiating a minefield—one wrong word, one misunderstood phrase, and the tension would snap like a wire.

Even later, as a mother herself, she brought these patterns into our home. Her compliance had been conditioned, layered over years of external control—from doctors who doubted her, to grandparents who wielded obedience as a weapon, to a mother-in-law whose dominance shaped my mum's every move. My mum didn't know any other way. Compliance had been survival. Saying no or asserting needs had always carried risk. And so, compliance became a quiet, internalised law, one she didn't even consciously question.

I saw the echoes of this compliance in myself long before I could name it. My own experiences with my ex, the sociopath who exploited my need for approval and fear of rejection, were amplified by this inherited conditioning. "Why didn't you just leave?" people would ask. As if, after a lifetime of being taught that your value is tied to obedience, stepping away is a simple choice. But it's not simple. Compliance wasn't a choice—it was survival encoded into the nervous system. My body had learned to defer, anticipate moods, and endure discomfort, carrying forward lessons from my mother's childhood into every relationship, long before my mind understood them.

The tension here is palpable in everyday life. Picture a kitchen on a Sunday morning, my mum bustling with tasks, her head spinning from residual neurological effects of encephalitis, her movements careful, cautious. My Nanna's words from decades earlier still echo in her mind: do as you're told, don't rock the boat, don't make anyone uncomfortable. Every minor decision—what to cook, how to respond to a request, even how to speak to me—carries a weight of past expectations, an invisible choreography of obedience and fear.

And it's not just behaviour. It's internalised fear, that subtle tightening in the chest when someone challenges you, the hesitation before expressing needs, the reflexive defence that comes long before the threat is real. Trauma doesn't just live in stories—it lives in bodies, in posture, in the way breath catches when conflict arises. My mum's brain and nervous system, shaped by illness and disbelief, by controlling adults and silent punishments, passed on a template to me. I learned to anticipate disappointment, to pre-empt conflict with compliance, and to measure every step against the possibility of rejection.

Reflecting on this, I see the invisible hand of transgenerational liability. Not a conscious punishment, not an intentional harm—but a structural echo, a pattern transmitted without words. Compliance becomes a survival strategy, a relational habit, a nervous system default. When unexamined, it can open doors to exploitation, as it did for me, as it could for my daughters if unaddressed.

And yet, within this tension, there is clarity. I recognise that my mum did the best she could with the tools she had, that her compliance was a strategy, not a moral failing. Understanding the "why" behind her behaviour does not excuse harm, but it illuminates the mechanics of inheritance: repeated fears, learned defensiveness, and relational patterns that accumulate silently across decades.

Cinematic snapshots come to mind: my mum in the living room, head spinning, trying to manage my childhood meltdowns while negotiating her own internal chaos. Me at eighteen, navigating the pressure to comply, to stay, to endure relationships that mirrored those I had witnessed growing up. My daughters, now, receiving the echoes of this inherited caution—not from cruelty, but from pattern. And I resolve, with every fibre of my being, that the chain stops here. That awareness, reflection, and conscious boundary-setting can interrupt this cycle of compliance, fear, and subtle coercion.

The suspense is in the quiet moments: the pause before saying no, the tightening in the chest when standing your ground, the invisible legacy pressing on the body, waiting for recognition. This is the inheritance of trauma—the unseen, cumulative weight of past generations shaping how we navigate the world, how we relate to others, how we perceive our own worth.

And still, there is hope. Striking in its own right, hope manifests in the small acts of defiance: asserting boundaries, naming the conditioning, teaching my daughters that their value is not negotiable. Every conscious choice to act from awareness rather than habit, every refusal to comply out of fear, creates a fissure in the inherited pattern. Every moment of attuned presence, every recognition of how these shadows operate, is a thread of light weaving through generations of conditioned compliance.

The tension, the suspense, the inherited fear—these are real, palpable, living in the bodies of each generation. But they are not immovable. They are scripts that can be read, understood, and rewritten. And in that revelatory recognition, there is power: the power to stop the transgenerational liability, to cultivate safety, to honour autonomy, and to instil resilience in the next generation.

Patterns run deep. They are often invisible, woven into the very way we breathe, react, and feel. What I have come to understand—and what my family history illustrates—is that trauma doesn't simply disappear when the moment ends. It passes through generations, carried in subtle habits, in body memory, in relational scripts that are silently learned and enforced. Recognising these cycles is the first step toward disrupting them.

Reflecting on my mother's childhood—the echoes of that white dress and impossible expectations—I see how compliance became a nervous system default. That blueprint became a framework for how she engaged with the world and, in turn, how I was raised. I learned to anticipate criticism, to measure my words, to suppress the parts of myself that might be inconvenient or unwelcome. I internalised the idea that survival often meant compliance, endurance, and invisibility. And these patterns, encoded in the nervous system, shaped my relationships and my sense of self-worth.

Intergenerational Trauma Intergenerational trauma travels silently—through stories, behaviours, and even biology. Science confirms it: extreme stress can influence gene expression, quietly priming descendants' nervous systems for vigilance or anxiety. In our family, the effects of my grandmother's harshness and my mother's early illness created nervous system patterns that were quietly inherited. I didn't consciously learn these behaviours—they felt innate. My body responded before my mind even understood the threat.

These inherited responses are a double-edged sword. They can protect, ensuring vigilance in dangerous situations. But when applied to everyday life, they amplify fear, shame, and over-compliance. For me, the lessons of survival turned into subtle anxiety, hyper-awareness of others' moods, and difficulty asserting boundaries. Every act of obedience was a whisper of past generations—an echo of what had kept them safe or controlled.

Environmental Influences Biology is only part of the story. Environmental cues and relational patterns reinforce inherited tendencies. The dynamics I witnessed in my mother's household, and later in my own home, demonstrated this clearly. Emotional suppression was rewarded. Defiance or neediness was punished. Compliance wasn't just expected—it was required.

These environmental reinforcements are powerful because they operate unconsciously. Children absorb them without realising it. We internalise rules, judgments, and fears as truths about ourselves. This is how low self-worth becomes a multi-generational inheritance. By adulthood, what started as external expectation has become internalised belief. I can trace my own insecurities and the fear of being "not enough" directly to these early patterns.

Recognising the Patterns Awareness is the gateway to change. I had to map the ways trauma had threaded through my family history, through my mother's experiences, my own conditioning, and the vulnerabilities it created in relationships.

One night, I remember sitting at the kitchen table with my mother. I told her, carefully, about the white dress and the punishment that followed. She recoiled, defensive. "She deserved it," she said. I felt the tension press against me like a physical weight. And yet, understanding the story, understanding the context, allowed me to separate my mother's intentions from the inherited patterns that affected both of us. This distinction is crucial: acknowledging trauma without excusing harm, recognising patterns without condemning ourselves.

Breaking the Cycle: Tools and Practices

• Self-reflection: notice triggers in body and mind.

• Boundaries: assert limits to recalibrate your nervous system.

• Attuned parenting: validate children's feelings without enforcing compliance.

• Mindfulness & journaling: observe patterns without judgment.

• Narrative reframing: rewrite inherited messages as affirmations of worth.

Attuned Parenting

Attuned parenting is a practical strategy to break inherited patterns. This isn't about perfection; it's about presence and responsiveness. It's about noticing the cues in your child's body, voice, and behaviour, and responding in ways that validate rather than control. By attuning to our children, we give them a nervous system blueprint of safety—something my mother and I lacked in our early years.

For example, if my daughter expresses fear or frustration, I sit with her, breathe with her, and acknowledge her feelings. I resist the urge to fix, to minimise, or to enforce compliance. Over time, this creates a sense of security that rewrites the default programming of anxiety and fear. Emotional regulation, attunement, and consistent validation act as buffers against inherited trauma.

Practical Tools for Transformation

Conscious strategies for interrupting cycles can include:

• **Reflective journaling:** Documenting triggers, responses, and patterns to gain clarity.

• **Mindfulness practices:** Breathing, body scans, and meditation to observe nervous system responses without judgment.

- **Therapeutic support:** Hypnotherapy, somatic therapy, and other modalities that address both body and mind.

- **Boundary-setting exercises:** Practicing saying no in safe contexts, gradually building comfort with self-assertion.

- **Narrative reframing:** Recognising inherited messages of inadequacy and consciously rewriting them as affirmations of inherent worth.

Each of these strategies interrupts automatic cycles. They create moments of choice where once there was only instinct, allowing the nervous system to gradually recalibrate from hypervigilance and compliance to resilience and attuned autonomy.

The Ripple Effect

Breaking cycles doesn't just affect the individual—it reshapes family dynamics. When I began asserting boundaries and modelling emotional awareness, my interactions with my mother, my partner, and my children changed. Patterns of criticism, defensiveness, and silent compliance softened. Responses became more attuned. Emotional validation increased. It wasn't instantaneous, but the shifts were tangible.

My daughters, witnessing these changes, absorbed a new template: their worth isn't conditional, their voices are safe, and their autonomy matters. In this way, conscious action has the power to create ripples across generations, disrupting patterns that once seemed immutable.

A Framework for Awareness

I have come to see this work as a framework of awareness, reflection, and action. It begins with recognising inherited patterns, understanding their origin, and observing how they manifest in present behaviour. It continues with conscious strategies: self-reflection, nervous system attunement, boundary-setting, and emotional validation. And it extends outward—through parenting, relationships, and mentorship—creating a supportive environment that reinforces new, healthier patterns.

The lesson is profound but simple: trauma may travel down generations, but it is not destiny. It can be interrupted, reshaped, and transformed. Awareness alone is not enough; intentional action is required. And yet, every small choice to break free from fear-based compliance, to nurture self-worth, and to model resilience strengthens the capacity for change in future generations.

Conclusion: Agency Amid Inheritance Inherited patterns shape us, but they are not destiny. Awareness gives insight, reflection brings clarity, and intentional action restores agency. Every boundary set, every voice heard, every act of attuned care is a thread of light breaking the cycle. The white dress no longer belongs to fear—it belongs to resilience.

Chapter 14: Epilogue – Thriving Beyond Fear

——

My body intelligence, my bio-infrastructure, my innate wisdom saying: "I've seen enough data.

I know the pattern.

I don't buy the story — I read the behaviour."

And that matters more than anything he has ever said.

Let me tell you the first thing you need to know...

The body never lies.

The nervous system is a scientist — it collects evidence.

It tracks tone, patterns, rupture, repair, safety signals, threat cues.

It remembers every cycle.

It knows when someone is dangerous, dismissive, or disconnected from empathy.

Words don't recalibrate your nervous system.

Behaviour does.

And his behaviour — across years — has shown a pattern of:

• empty apologies

• temporary calm

• re-escalation

• manipulation

- no integration

- no ownership

- no remorse that leads to repair

That's not "oops, I stuffed up."

That's strategic — or habitual — self-preservation without empathy.

Apologies without change = emotional manipulation

Science proves it. Real remorse shows up in the body through:

- consistent action, not words

- lowered aggression

- true empathy

- accountability

- repair

No repair. No belief. Your body knows.When those don't appear — not once in 28 years —

your body moves from hope into survival mode.

This is why your body intelligence is lighting up like a warning flare.

My system isn't confused.

It's wise.

It's reading the chemistry of unmet promises and watching for danger patterns.

My body doesn't believe it because it learned the truth.

I didn't "give up."

I didn't "stop trusting."

I evolved out of illusion.

That's what healing looks like.

That's what authenticity looks like.

That's what nervous-system awakening feels like.

I'm not responding to his stories anymore —

I'm responding to the data.

And here's the powerful reframe:

If my body doesn't believe his remorse...

that means my body is finally moving out of freeze and fantasy

and back into strength and clarity.

That's my baseline calling me home.

That's safety choosing me.

I want to ask you something, and I want you to answer with your body intelligence, not your brain:

When your body says "I don't believe him," does it feel like fear...

or does it feel like relief?

Take a breath and feel it.

I'm right here with you.

REFERENCE

Bancroft, L., *Kids who side with the Abuser, Part 1*, viewed 7 December 2025, <https://lundybancroft.com/kids-who-side-with-the-abuser-part-1/>

Bancroft, L. *Kids who side with the Abuser, Part 2*, viewed 7 December 2025, <https://lundybancroft.com/kids-who-side-with-the-abuser-part-2/>

Ogden, P., 2015, *Sensorimotor Psychotherapy: Interventions for trauma and attachment*, W. W. Norton & Company, New York

Schore, A. N., 2019, *The development of the unconscious mind*, W. W. Norton & Company, New York

The Social Being 28 August 2025, *Don't Raise Obedient Girls*, online video, viewed 30 November 2025, <https://www.youtube.com/shorts/Z2obPrKzE-wA>

www.ingramcontent.com/pod-product-compliance
Lightning Source LLC
Chambersburg PA
CBHW070806050426
42452CB00011B/1914